TWAYNE'S WORLD AUTHORS SERIES

A Survey of the World's Literature

Sylvia E. Bowman, Indiana University

GENERAL EDITOR

France

Maxwell A. Smith, Guerry Professor of French, Emeritus
The University of Chattanooga
Visiting Professor in Modern Languages
The Florida State University

EDITOR

Jacques Prévert

(TWAS 24)

TWAYNE'S WORLD AUTHORS SERIES (TWAS)

The purpose of TWAS is to survey the major writers —novelists, dramatists, historians, poets, philosophers, and critics—of the nations of the world. Among the national literatures covered are those of Australia, Canada, China, Eastern Europe, France, Germany, Greece, India, Italy, Japan, Latin America, New Zealand, Poland, Russia, Scandinavia, Spain, and the African nations, as well as Hebrew, Yiddish, and Latin Classical literatures. This survey is complemented by Twayne's United States Authors Series and English Authors Series

The intent of each volume in these series is to present a critical-analytical study of the works of the writer; to include biographical and historical material that may be necessary for understanding, appreciation, and critical appraisal of the writer; and to present all material in clear, concise English—but not to vitiate the scholarly content of the work by doing so.

Jacques Prévert

By WILLIAM E. BAKER

Twayne Publishers, Inc.   ::   New York

Preface

Something rather unusual in modern literature occurred when the poetry of Jacques Prévert was first collected and published in 1946: all kinds of people—not just students and professors—began reading poems. They have kept on reading Prévert, with the result that in the last fifteen years he has become the most popular poet in France. His first collection of poems, *Paroles,* has already sold over 675,000 copies; and subsequent works, *Spectacle* (1951) and *La Pluie et le beau temps* (1955), have sold together another 575,000 copies.[1] Since Victor Hugo, no French poet has had such an impact on the public.

Before 1946 Prévert had of course been known as a brilliant film-scenario writer, but his poems had appeared only occasionally in various periodicals. According to rumor, during the occupation many early poems passed from hand to hand in type-written form, or *de bouche à oreille*.[2] Upon the appearance of *Paroles,* however, Prévert established himself as a major poet—some say *the* major poet of his generation.

> Henceforth none deny that Jacques Prévert
> is our national poet. . . .[3]

Even more shocking, Prévert earned widespread acclaim from influential critics. Shocking indeed—for popular poetry in France had grown synonymous with banal verse of little esthetic merit. Critics in the tradition of the late Symbolists were prone to make this a priori assumption an integral part of their poetic doctrine:

A poetry which wishes to rise to a high level cannot direct itself to a very numerous public.[4]

One esteemed, conservative critic, Thierry Maulnier, very succinctly summed up the temper of poetry and criticism in France before World War II.

[5]

Nothing is more foreign to French life than a French poem. The most popular English or German poets are the greatest English or German poets. The most popular French poets have been our worst poets.[5]

Gaetan Picon, writing in *Panorama de la nouvelle littérature française*, concludes that according to Maulnier's orthodox dogma it is impossible for a poet to be both popular and good. Banality, cheapness—badness, in fact—are frankly identified with popularity. Thus Maulnier believed that there was an unbridgeable chasm between the talented poet and the people, and that this arrangement developed with the indifferent consent of the best poets.

. . . popular favor is, in France, almost always withdrawn from poets who not only scorn to solicit the approval of their nation, but even refuse to cast an eye on the greatest moments of its destiny, to welcome into their works a reflection of its sufferings or its glory.[6]

Prévert, Picon suggests, may upset this theory. Although little known to literary critics before 1940, Prévert's name would now arouse controversy only if it were absent from an anthology of major poets of this century. Speaking of the work of Michaux, Char, and Prévert, Picon claims that ". . . it is no longer possible to ignore the importance of these works."[7] The uniqueness of Prévert, then, seems to be that he is both popular *and* good.

The question is no longer "Why study this man Prévert?" but rather "Why has he not been studied?" The poet's reputation in France is such that he is mentioned simultaneously with Jean-Paul Sartre as one of the major twentieth century revolutionary writers. Queneau states flatly that the two "great leaders of youth" in the 1940's were Sartre and Prévert, and the two principal books *Paroles* and *l'Être et le néant* (*Being and Nothingness*).[8] Brodin, too, classes them together as "great leaders."[9]

In America, however, Prévert is largely neglected.[10] In the first place, both he and his poems perhaps shock those who think of Eliot and *The Waste Land* when they think of modern poetry. He does not resemble in any way the stereotype of a pure poet, the solitary intellectual steeped in books; neither is he quite a bohemian, the savage inspired chiefly by drugs and sex. With the latter type, traditionally represented by Rimbaud, Baudelaire, or Jarry, he shares certain attitudes; but though he can attack social institutions with pungent satire and can manifest a definite fondness for women and wine, Prévert seldom flaunts his scorn for social codes and artistic traditions as the Dadaists and early Surrealists did, merely to scandalize. His poetry also lacks any hint of that secular mysticism so noticeable in his contemporaries. What he writes can be grotesque or absurd, deliberately so, but he is never pretentious.

Prévert also does some things American poets with prestige would probably never do, and he doesn't do other things they always seem to do. For example, Prévert writes and illustrates children's books, and allows his poems to be recorded as popular songs, but he never writes essays of formal literary criticism. He scribbles pure buffoonery, low puns, and ribaldry, but employs no Greek epigraphs to gild such pranks. His constant subjects are France and the French of today; for history and mythology he has only amused contempt. He is not, usually, the subject of his own poems. There is, in short, no modern American poetry very much like Prévert's poetry and no respected modern American poet much like Prévert.

The man dresses, according to the accounts of friends, like a tramp (*un voyou*),[11] yet his diction includes not only street obscenities but phrases of great poise and delicacy. He seems to avoid literary society and teaches at no university, preferring the company of *copains* in cafés. He writes atheist and pro-Communist diatribes in the most direct, unsubtle and insulting manner conceivable, yet often his lighter verse falls into infantile sentimentality. He hates war but condones revolution. Whatever is academic or intellectual he scorns, but he uses a vocabulary of immense scope.

The list of apparent paradoxes could be extended, since paradox is characteristic of both his material and his style. But such a list reveals that the contradictions of Prévert remain consistent and reflect an unchanging set of attitudes—or prejudices. Against the Catholic Church, for example, Prévert levels his most acrimonious satire; he wages a bitter, one-man campaign against the entire institution from the Pope down to the humblest believer. Nevertheless, the poet professes many "Christian" virtues: charitable love for the poor and wronged and for children, respect for labor but not for riches, belief in harmony between man and nature, and a reverence for animals rivaling that of Saint Francis.

Such attitudes or prejudices make tidy categories: the "anti" poems, written about things the poet is against; the "pro" poems, written about things he favors; and a small group of documentary or "slice-of-life" poems, written about almost anything. Given that the poet interprets his world largely in sharp blacks and whites, it is useful to study Prévert not as a "proletarian" poet, but as an anti-bourgeois and pro-proletariat poet; the one prefix suggests the vitriol that saturates so many poems on capitalism, and the other, the sachet that accompanies the poems written about common people. A few poems, on the other hand, strive for an unusual, cinematic objectivity. In the first chapters I have taken up all three categories both singly and in relation to one another.

It is Prévert's handling of the French language, however, rather than the fierceness of his convictions, that will most likely establish an enduring reputation. His styles are unique without being intricate and mannered. He ignites upon occasion a fantastic display of verbal fireworks: puns, alliteration, obsessive rhyme, tongue slips and coined words. Elsewhere he speaks in simple, straightforward idiom, and often there are finely chiseled images presented in subdued, graceful cadences. In chapters 4-7 I point out the dominant characteristics of Prévert's language and suggest the esthetic values his poetry implies. In the last chapter I turn to the implications of Prévert's attitudes toward poetry and language for modern American literature.

Always, the poet's aim seems to be communication rather than mystification. He does not ask the reader to achieve rarefied states of consciousness by contemplating symbols drawn from highly esoteric sources; he asks one merely to look at the everyday world with an unjaded eye. To look and to feel rather than to cogitate—this is the message implicit throughout Prévert's work. His is a poetry of searing images, music both raucous and refined, and humorous chatter; at its best this poetry can evoke a world of marvels—marvels experienced rather than comprehended intellectually, marvels found nowhere but in the glorious chaos of everyday life.

Translator's Note

Throughout this volume, and in the Appendix (p. 133), the reader will find translations of a representative selection of Prévert's poetry, along with the original French versions. A few observations on the purpose and method of these translations are perhaps in order. Many translators offer one of two reasons for what they do: they are zestful scholars who enjoy the most demanding mental gymnastics, or they are perfectionists, unable to resist the challenge of the impossible. The perfect translation, goes the commonplace, is indeed forever impossible. By a universal agreement among all who know more than one tongue, no translation can ever yield the "flavor" of the original. The translator's preface, an elaborate apology, is for the purpose of reaffirming his belief in that agreement. One ordinarily adds a mention of his modest aims in the face of these overwhelming, inherent difficulties, and finishes with a deprecatory remark or two on the inevitable transcience of all things linguistic.

Very well. A perfect translation, whatever that may be, is impossible. But surely good ones are not. Admittedly, one must forever sacrifice meaning for music, or the other way about, but it is time, I think, to refrain from bemoaning the fact further. One simply cannot help the original sin of those ancestors who sundered the *Ursprache*. Attempting a very good translation—a feasible if immodest goal—can still serve a very practical end: it forces one to learn the resources not only of a poem and a poet, but of two languages, two cultures. Moreover, the translator learns not merely by analyzing, but by creating as well. Translation, then, is more than an exercise, more than the acceptance of a "challenge"; it is a highly rewarding kind of study.

Prévert often writes as one talks, and an English version of him ought to sound like an English-speaking person speaking English. True, Prévert's profanity, slang and proverb often have

no exact equivalents in English; but the substitutes one uses
ought to be, at the very least, native expressions of the same
classification. The meaning may even be of less importance than
the *kind* of expression employed and its impact in context. The
very powerful poem *Barbara*, for example, comes to a climax
with the expression "Quelle connerie la guerre." To translate
more or less literally would produce a bizarre, un-English curse
—one too pungent, besides, to convey just the right degree of
shock. Translating a poet like Prévert involves more than searching for synonyms. Ideally, one also learns two cultures from top
to bottom—especially the bottom.

Thus, paradoxically, many of these poems depend so much on
peculiarities of the French language that to translate them one
must choose phrases which are peculiarly English. The "meaning" gets lost, of course, but some of the "flavor" is perhaps pre-
served. Prévert's line "Ceux qui debout les morts" in *Dinner
of Heads* thus became "Those who over the top," since both cries
were used in World War I to launch charges from the trenches.
Even so, in *Dinner of Heads*, it has been necessary all too often
to rely on notes in order to explain allusions for which no familiar
English analogues could be found. The reference to the statue of
the carrier pigeon, the "Pigeon-Soldat," with its subdued play
on the word "pigeon" ("sucker" in English) would probably
mean nothing to most American readers. This reference belongs
to a chain of bird images which includes the "colombophile" who
heaved the water pitcher. Doubtless the Audubon Society would
be a recognizable equivalent of the French Society of Colombo-
philes, but substituting a reference to the former would destroy
the pun on the President's "Columbus Egg head." Also, the
many proverbs to which Prévert gives an ironic twist do not
always have an English counterpart; whenever such a counterpart was available, however, I used it, historical incongruities
notwithstanding. The poet's delight in poking fun at the saws of
his culture could not be rendered otherwise.

The easiest pieces to work with were those in which Prévert
presents a series of very concrete, specific images. One finds
such images in the haiku-like *Alicante* and in *Inventory*. Often
a translator has trouble with a word like *mentalité*, *Gemüt-
lichkeit*, or *res* because such words contain so many possible
nuances, depending on the context. But a word like "raccoon"

will have a fairly exact, unambiguous equivalent wherever raccoons are found. Sometimes, however, even very specific words
carry an additional, untranslatable meaning. The word *armoire
à glace*, sounding as if it ought to mean ice box but being, in
English, a closet with a mirror on the door, forces one to aban-
don a bilingual Prévert poem in which the author intends the
mistranslation. And the outrageous pun "De deux choses lune/
l'autre c'est le soleil" defeats a translator at the very beginning
of *Le Paysage Changeur*. The same is true of the final line of
La Transcendance—"Âme haine!"

Some works were thus rejected immediately as too difficult
to translate. Other fine poems were discarded because they
treated essentially the same theme and treated it in the same
way as a poem more readily rendered into English. All but one
of the poems come from *Paroles*, because that book still seems
Prévert's best. It is nevertheless regrettable that space does not
permit an extensive selection from *Spectacle*, to give the reader
an idea of Prévert's ingenuity as a screen writer; for works like
La Tour are indeed a novel kind of dramatic literature.

I hope to have included enough poems to illustrate liberally
my remarks and to give readers some of Prévert's variety, while
maintaining his balance. In the translations I have also tried to
transmit some of this elusive "flavor" of the original. No doubt
I have failed often, but students of the language will, I trust, be
moved enough by admiration for the original to rectify my
shortcomings.

Acknowledgments

To the young French girl—the name is long since forgotten—who lent me my first copy of *Paroles*, I remain profoundly grateful. Her compatriots have also helped to revise my translations; Mme. Nadia Burkett and M. Pierre Weisz, especially, caught numerous errors and oversights. Those that remain are my own responsibility. Frank Jones, at the University of Washington, gave me encouragement at the outset of this study; and Merrill F. Heiser, at the University of Hawaii, provided advice and good cheer during the writing of the first draft. The preparation of the final text was greatly expedited by the editorial and secretarial skills of Miss Julie Saunders.

I am of course above all grateful to Jacques Prévert and to the editors of Gallimard for permission to publish translations as well as original versions of several poems. René Bertelé of Gallimard also kindly supplied biographical data about Prévert. Finally, I wish to thank the following publishers for permission to quote from works still in copyright: The Mercure de France, for passages in Jean Queval's *Jacques Prévert*; The Museum of Modern Art for Picasso's remarks quoted in Alfred H. Barr, Jr.'s *Picasso: Forty Years of His Art*; and the *French Review* for excerpts from Albert Gaudin's "La Poésie de Jacques Prévert."

Contents

Contents

Chronology

1900 Jacques Prévert born February 4 at Neuilly-sur-Seine.

1905- Attends public schools in Paris.
1914

1915 Begins earning his livelihood at various odd jobs.

1920 Military service; Prévert stationed first at Lunéville, where
      he meets Yves Tanguy the painter, then at Constantinople,
      where he meets Marcel Duhamel. Returning to Paris, all
      three take lodgings on the Rue du Château.

1925 Meets the Surrealists (Breton, Aragon, Péret, Desnos,
      Leiris, Queneau, etc.), who are frequent visitors at the
      Rue du Château.

1930 The first poems by Prévert appear in various reviews:
      Souvenirs de famille ou l'Ange garde-chiourme, in *Bifur*.
      The following year, *Tentative de description d'un dîner
      de têtes à Paris-France*, in *Commerce*.

1932- Prévert works with the theater company "Groupe Oc-
1936 tobre," writing plays in which he often takes a role him-
      self. In 1933, he travels with this company to Moscow to
      present his *La Bataille de Fontenoy* for an international
      congress of the Worker's Theater. During this same peri-
      od, Prévert begins writing film scenarios and popular
      songs rendered by Agnès Capri and Marianne Oswald,
      among others.

1932 *L'Affaire est dans le sac*, film written with Pierre Prévert.

1935 *Le Crime de monsieur Lange*, film written with Jean
      Renoir.

1936 *La Crosse en l'air* appears in *Soutes*.

1937 *Drôle de drame*, film written with Marcel Carné.

1938 Visit to the United States. *Quai des brumes*, film written with Marcel Carné. *Disparus de Saint-Agil*, film written with Christian Jaque and Pierre Laroche.

1939 *Le Jour se lève*, film written with Marcel Carné.

1942 *Les Visiteurs du soir*, film written with M. Carné and P. Laroche.

1943 *Adieu, Leonard*, film written with Pierre Prévert. *Lumière d'été*, film written with Jean Grémillon. *Les Enfants du paradis*, film written with Marcel Carné.

1945 *Les Portes de la nuit*, film written with Marcel Carné. *Aubervilliers*, film written with Eli Lotar. First performance of Prévert's *Le Rendez-vous*, ballet with music by J. Kosma, choreography by R. Petit, curtain by Picasso, photographic decor by Brassaï, at the Sarah-Bernhardt theater. *C'est à Saint-Paul-de-Vence* . . . , preface to *Souvenirs du présent* by André Verdet.

1946 *Paroles*, first collection of Prévert's poems. *Le Cheval de Trois*, with poems also by Verdet and André Virel. *Histoires*, written in collaboration with André Verdet, illustrated by Mayo. *Poèmes*, collection with sketches by Brassaï. *Voyage-surprise*, film with Pierre Prévert. Birth of Prévert's daughter Michèle.

1947 *Contes pour enfants pas sages*, illustrated by Elsa Henriquez. *Paroles*, new edition, revised and augmented. *Le Petit Lion*, with photos by Ylla.

1948 Prévert suffers severe injuries in a fall at the office of the Radiodiffusion Nationale, Champs-Elysées. After several weeks in a coma, he recovers, moves to Saint-Paul-de-Vence, where he remains with his wife and child for some years.

1949 *C'est à Saint-Paul-de-Vence* . . . , new edition with cover by Emilienne Delacroix. *Paroles*, Le Point du Jour-N.R.F. edition.

1950   *Le Bergère et le ramoneur*, film cartoon with Paul Grimault. *Des bêtes . . .*, with photos by Ylla.

1951   *Spectacle*, new collection of poetry and dramatic works. *Vignette pour les vignerons*, with sketches by Françoise Gilot and photos by Marianne. *Le Grand Bal du printemps*, with photos by Izis.

1952   *Bim, le petit âne*, with photos by Albert Lamorisse. *Charmes de Londres*, with photos by Izis. *Lettre des îles Baladar*, with drawings by André François. *Guignol*, with drawings by Elsa Henriquez.

1953   *Tour de chant*, with illustrations by Loris and music by Christiane Verger. *L'Opéra de la lune*, sketches by Jacqueline Duhême and music by Christiane Verger.

1955   *La Pluie et le beau temps*, collection of poetry. *Lumière d'homme*. Prévert returns to Paris.

1956   *Miro*, written with G. Ribemont-Dessaignes.

1957   Exhibition of Prévert's collages at Adrien Maeght Gallery. *Images*, Prévert's art introduced by René Bertelé.

1959   *Portraits de Picasso*, photos by André Villers.

1963   *Histoires, et d'autres histoires*, enlarged edition.

Jacques Prévert

CHAPTER 1

"Pro" and *"Anti"* Themes

A NY reader with a passable knowledge of French can look through a small selection of Prévert's poetry and discern the author's major themes. His topics and the emotions they arouse in him are unmistakably plain. A number of critics have listed them in a paragraph or less, writing in most cases about the first and most popular collection, *Paroles*; but the lists could serve for almost all his work.

On reading the poems in this collection [*Paroles*] one quickly becomes aware of dominant themes that appear and reappear throughout. Prévert reveals himself as an enemy of social and economic injustice. He hates war. He launches bitter attacks against religious insincerity. On the positive side, he loves nature, city streets, people, animals, and birds. His love poems, though not romantic, are as moving as any that are being written today.[1]

The sun, children, women (preferably young ones), simple and natural people, animals (wild ones rather than tame)—these are the heroes of Prévert's poems, and his comedy is made complete by their adversaries: priests, generals, intellectuals, guardian angels, all oppressors.[2]

The second list quoted above is the more informative, for Prévert does not attack abstractions like "social and economic injustice," or "religious insincerity"; he names names—the Pope of the Catholic Church, Maréchal Pétain and the French colonial government in Viet Nam,[3] for example. Whatever generalizations a critic may use to cover Prévert's subject matter, they will be inevitably somewhat false to the poetry, which remains specific.

One group of themes can be called the "anti" group. Here one finds poems or parts of poems devoted to the ridicule of the bourgeoisie, the Church, militarists and chauvinists, academicians and, as Queneau says, "all oppressors." Anti-bourgeoisie, anti-Church, anti-militarist, and anti-intellectual: such is Prévert's stance vis-à-vis the conventional structure of his society.

A second group of themes tempers the acid of the satirist with the honey of the lyrical poet. These are the "pro" themes, in which the poet expresses repeatedly his sympathy and praise for the proletariat—a group of character types having the virtues of honesty, courage, and brotherly affection in contrast to the vices of the moneyed class; he exalts free, unfettered love between man and woman; he finds kinship and harmony between nature and the natural, uncivilized spirit of man; he celebrates the life of the senses and admires the imaginative *élan* of the child.

Of course in the poetry one discovers that Prévert identifies the bourgeoisie with greed, pompousness, and insensitivity and the proletariat with fraternity, honesty and courage. But these attributes would remain tiresome vacuities unless attached to people, so Prévert selects or invents characters whom he can admire or strike at. Thus, returning to the two lists quoted previously, one may agree that Prévert hates war only if one adds that the poet hates it in the form of the militarists and politicians who cause it.

Here the poet's training as a film writer seems to have influenced his poetry, which often consists of a dramatization of character types. Indeed, many of the "poems" contained in the collection *Spectacle* (a noun meaning "show") are dramatic sketches which have been or could be presented on the stage. Jean Queval, who has studied this writer's film art more thoroughly than any other critic,[4] finds in Prévert's thirty-odd film scripts as in his poetry the same sharp distinction between character types: they are either heroes or villains, good or bad guys.

Thus recur, from film to film, under varying sorts of direction, the same puppet show, the same tragedy, the same poetry. The same characters recur: good and bad; in love and unhappy; natural children of the earth which is a celestial body, and monsters complicated and vicious, beings twisted by some trauma, and determined by it. One will see that they double—or redouble—from one film to the next if not within the same one, but each fully complete, and shaped from a single kind of clay. The same characters, who take form and significance through contrast; characters who do not change, do not evolve.[5]

These same invariable, morally static characters appear throughout the three collections of poetry. As Queval suggests, they are like puppets in a Punch-and-Judy show, acting perennially the same role though costumes and sets may change. And the cinema provides also an analogy to Prévert's technique. Like a selective cameraman, he records many different individuals at many different moments, yet makes each event another symbol of the same, simple, eternal, human idiocies and glories.

One of Prévert's early long poems, *Tentative de description d'un dîner de têtes à Paris-France*, can illustrate these themes treated at length. Despite an element of calculated absurdity and the great verve and wit with which it develops, the work is serious satire, a good example of *littérature engagée*. Picon believes that the poem is a mainstay of Prévert's reputation in this genre. "To be sure, he is a great satiric poet; and *The Dinner of Heads*, in its extraordinary power of invective and its vengeful violence, is without equal in our literature."[6] Also, Queval notes, *The Dinner of Heads* makes up a small, complete anthology of the poet's themes, his ideals, and his pet prejudices.

All that he has to tell us is already in the first poem of his first volume, in *Dinner of Heads* where one reads, written in the same form, with the same movement, and so to speak at the same pace, the curse hurled at capitalist ownership and insistence that life be lived fully and according to the *natural order*, far from contemporary civilization if necessary, on islands if need be. Each must be given his island of the birds.[7]

To illustrate the poet's gift for satire, then, as well as to show how he expresses his deepest convictions, the complete text of the poem is given on the following pages, both in translation and in the original.

AN ENDEAVOR TO DESCRIBE A DINNER OF HEADS
AT PARIS-FRANCE[*]

Those who piously . . .[A]
Those who copiously . . .
Those who tricolor
Those who inaugurate
Those who believe
Those who believe they believe
Those who caw-caw[B]
Those who have quills
Those who eke out
Those who andromache
Those who dreadnought
Those who uppercase
Those who sing in time
Those who brush to a shine
Those who have a paunch
Those who drop their eyes
Those who can carve chicken
Those who are bald on the inside of their head
Those who bless the pack
Those who ride to hounds
Those who over the top
Those who . .x bayonets
Those who give cannons to children
Those who give children to cannons
Those who stand united and do not fall divided[C]
Those who know a hawk from a handsaw
Those whose giant's wings keep them from flying[D]
Those who in dreams plant shards of broken bottles on the great wall
   of China
Those who put a wolf over their face when they eat mutton
Those who steal eggs and who dare not cook them
Those who have fifteen thousand seven hundred and eighty-one feet
   of Mount Blanc, nine hundred and eighty-four of Eiffel Tower, ten
   inches around the chest and are proud of it
Those who suckle on France[E]
Those who run, fly and avenge us,[F] all those and a lot of others
   proudly entered the presidential palace at Elysée, crunching gravel
   underfoot, all of them shoved one another, hurried, because there

[*] Original French text of this translation appears on page 133.

was a grand festival of swelled heads and each one had made up the one he wanted.

One a clay pipe head, another an English admiral's head, there were some with stink bomb heads, Gallifet heads,[G] heads of animals sick in the head,[H] Auguste Comte heads, Rouget de Lisle heads, Saint Theresa heads, heads of head cheese, foot heads, monseigneur heads and milkman heads.

Some, to make everyone laugh, wore their charming calf faces, and they were such dears and so sad, with little green grass spears in the crevices of their ears like seaweed in the crevices of rocks, that no one noticed them.

A mother in a death's head laughingly showed off her daughter with an orphan's head to the old friend-of-the-family diplomat who had made himself a Jack-the-Ripper head.[1]

It was really exquisitely charming and of such good taste that when the President arrived with a sumptuous Columbus egg head it was positively ecstatic.

"It was simple, but you had to think of it," said the President unfolding his napkin and face to face with so much malice and simple grace the guests could not quell the swell of their emotion; through the eyes of his cardboard crocodile mask a big industrialist sheds real tears of joy, a littler one gnaws the table, pretty women rub their breasts very delicately and the admiral, carried away by his enthusiasm, drinks his goblet of champagne from the wrong side, munches the stem of the goblet and, intestine perforated, dies erect, clinging to the rail of his chair crying: "Children first!"

Odd coincidence, the wife of the shipwrecked, upon the advice of her maid, had that very morning outfitted herself with an astonishing war-widow's head, with two large wrinkles of bitterness on each side of her mouth and two little gray hollows of sadness under her blue eyes.

Standing on her chair, she hails the President and demands in loud cries a military pension and the right to wear on her evening gown the sextant of the deceased as a Saint Andrew's cross.

Calmed down a little, she next lets her look of a lonely woman wander over the table and seeing among the hors-d'oeuvres some smoked herring, she takes some, not caring, with tearful bearing, then gets the rest, thinking of the admiral who, as a living guest, wasn't so obsessed with their zest and nevertheless thought them the best. Stop. The chief of protocol now says that the eating must stop because the President is going to speak.

The President has risen, he has broken the crown of his eggshell with his knife so as to be a little less warm, just a little bit less warm.

He speaks and the silence is such that flies are heard buzzing about and they can be heard so distinctly buzzing about that the President can no longer be heard at all, and this is certainly too bad because he is speaking about flies, precisely, and about their incontestable utility in all areas, and in the colonial area especially.

". . . Because without flies, no fly swatters, without fly swatters no Dey in Algiers, no consulate—no insults to avenge,[1] no olive trees, no Algeria, no heat waves, gentlemen, and heat waves are what saves the tourist's health . . ."

But when flies get bored they die, and all this business about the old days, all these statistics filling them with a profound sadness, they begin by letting loose one small foot from the ceiling, then the other, and fall like flies, in the plates—on shirt fronts, dying like flies, as the saying is.

"The most noble conquest of man is the horse," says the President, "and I regret that I have but one to give to my country."

This is the end of the address; like a gutted orange thrown splat against the wall by an ill-bred brat the MARSEILLAISE erupts and all the spectators, spattered with vert-de-gris and brasses, arise, stuffed to the eyes, drunk with the History of France and Pontet-Canet.

All are standing, except the man with a Rouget de Lisle[K] head who believes that it is all over and who finds that after all it isn't so badly executed and then, little by little, the music has subsided and the mother with a death's head has taken advantage of this and pushed her little girl with an orphan's head toward the President.

Flowers in hand, the child begins her compliment: "Monsieur President . . ." but the emotion, the heat, the flies, so there she wavers and there she falls with her face in the flowers, her teeth clenched like a pair of shears.

The man with a herniary bandage head and the man with a carbuncle head rush forward, and the little one is lifted up, autopsied, and denied by her mother, who, finding on the child's program some obscene sketches such as one doesn't often see, doesn't dare believe that it was the friend-of-the-family diplomat on whom the father's position depends who amused himself so lightly.

Hiding the program in her dress, she pricks her breast with the little white pencil and emits a long howl, and her grief is painful to see for those who think that here is certainly most assuredly the agony of a mother who has lost her child.

Proud to be looked at, she lets herself go, she gives herself to her audience, she moans, she chants:

"Where then is my little darling girl, where is she then, my little

Barbara who used to give grass to the bunnies and the bunnies to cobras?"

But the President, who is probably not at the stage of the loss of the first offspring, motions with his hand and the festival begins again.

And those who had come to sell coal and wheat sell coal and wheat and big islands surrounded on all sides by seas, big islands with rubber tire trees and pianos metallic and finely styled so that one may not hear very much of the screams of the natives around the plantations when the smart-alecky colonists try out their semiautomatics after dinner.

One bird upon their shoulder, another inside their blouse, a grouse they will have roasted a little later at their house, the poets come and go in all the salons.

"It's really quite a success," says one of them, but amid popping flash bulbs the chief of protocol is caught evermore and red-handed in a misdemeanor, stirring a cup of iced chocolate too soon and with a coffee spoon.

"There isn't any special spoon for the iced chocolate, as there is for gravy, it's crazy," says the secretary, "They ought to have thought of it, the dentist has his tooth-puller, the paper its paper-cutter and red radishes their radish butter."

But suddenly all is atremble because a man with a man's head has passed in, a man whom no one asked in and who places gently on the table the head of Louis XVI in a basket.

Truly it is a horrible sight; teeth, old men and doors clatter with fright.

"We are lost, we have beheaded a locksmith!" howl the merchants of Calais, sliding down the bannister, sliding down in their nightgown, gray like cape Gris-Nez is gray.

The horrible sight, the tumult, the discomfort, the taking of the cake, the state of siege and outside in a grand uniform, black hands under white gloves, the sentry who sees in the streams of blood and on his tunic a stink bug thinks that things are going badly and a man must get away if there is still time.

"I would have liked," said the man, smiling, "to bring you also the remains of the imperial family, which repose, they say, in the Caucasian cavern, Rue Pigalle, but the Cossacks who cry, dance and sell drinks keep a jealous watch over their dead.

"You can't have everything; I'm not Ruy Blas, I'm not Cagliostro, I don't have a crystal ball, I don't have tea leaves, I don't have the cotton-wad beard of those who prophesy, I enjoy very much laughing in a social way, I speak here for the bedridden, I monologue for the longshoremen, I phonograph for splendid dolts from skid row, and it is entirely by chance that I visit you in your little inner circle.

"The first one to say: in a pig's eye! is a dead man. No one says so, he's mistaken, it was for laughs.

"You have the right to laugh a little and if you wanted I would take you to visit the city, but you are afraid to go, you know what you know, that the Tower of Pisa is leaning and that you get vertigo when you yourself are leaning over the terraces of cafes below.

"And nevertheless you would be very much entertained, like the President when he descends into the mines, like little Pip all dressed up when he goes to see Newgate, like when you were a child and they took you to the Zoological Gardens to see the great ant-eater.

"You would have been able to see the bums without a beggar's corner, the lepers without bells, shirtless men sleeping on benches, sleeping for a moment, because it is prohibited to stay there for very long.

"You would have seen men in the asylums of night making the sign of the cross in order to have a bed, and the families with eight children 'who are cooped up eight in one room' and if you had been good you would have had the good fortune and the pleasure to see the father who gets up because of chronic fits, the mother who dies quietly on her last child, the rest of the family who run away and who try to escape their misery by clearing a road in blood.

"You must see it, I tell you, it is exciting, you must see when the good Shepherd conducts to Villette slaughterhouse his flock, when the son of the family is sowing his wild oats with a soft sound on the sidewalk, when the children who are bored change beds in their dormitory building, you must see the man asleep in his cage-bed when his alarm is about to ring.

"Look at him, listen to him snore, he dreams, he dreams he is leaving on a trip, dreams that everything is going fine, dreams that he has a window seat, but the alarm clock pointer meets the one on the transit line and the man erect from a slumber plunges his face in a basin of water, icy in the winter, fetid in the summer.

"Look at him hurrying, drinking his coffee, going into the factory, working, but he isn't awake yet, the alarm didn't ring long enough, the coffee wasn't strong enough; he is still dreaming, dreaming he is on a trip, dreaming he has a window seat, leaning through the doorway and falling into a garden, falling into a cemetery, waking up and shrieking like an animal, missing two fingers, the machine chewed him, he wasn't there to dream and as you could guess that had to happen.

"You even think that this isn't the ordinary thing and that one swallow doesn't make the spring, you think that an earth tremor in New Guinea doesn't prevent the vine's growing in France, the cheeses' ripening or the earth's turning.

"But I didn't ask you to think; I told you to look, to listen, so as to get in the habit of it, so as not to be surprised to hear your billiard balls crack the day the real elephants come back to reclaim their ivory.

"Because that head, so faintly alive, that you move under dead pasteboard, that pale head under the funny pasteboard, that head with all its wrinkles, all its trained grimaces, one day you will shake it off your trunk with a detached air and when it falls in the sawdust you will say neither yes nor no.

"And if it is not you it will be some of yours, because you know the stories about birds of a feather and it isn't cerebral ware you lack.

"I'm kidding, but you know, like the fellow says, a mere nothing is enough to put things on different roads, a little gun cotton in the ear of a sick monarch and the monarch explodes. The queen runs to his bedside. There isn't any more bedside. There isn't any more palace. All is rather ruin and grief. The queen senses her mind beginning to slip and sink. To comfort her an unknown with a nice smile gives her bad coffee to drink.[L] The queen takes it, the queen dies of it and servants stick tickets on the children's baggage. The man with the nice smile comes back, opens the biggest trunk, pushes the little princes inside, puts the padlock on the trunk, the trunk in storage, and withdraws, rubbing his hands.

"And when I say, Monsieur President, Ladies and Gentlemen, the King, the Queen, the little princes, I do it to cover things generally, because you can't reasonably blame regicides who don't have a king at hand if they sometimes exercise their talents in their immediate surroundings.

"Particularly among those who think that a handful of rice is enough to feed a whole Chinese family for long years.

"Among ladies who sneer at exhibits because a black woman carries a black child on her back, and who have carried for six or seven months in their white belly a child that is white and dead.

"Among the thirty thousand sensible people composed of one soul and one body who paraded on the sixth of March at Brussels, military music out in front, before the monument erected to the Soldier Pigeon and among those who will parade tomorrow at Brive-la-Gaillarde,[M] at Rosa-the-Rose or at Carpa-la-Juive[N] before the monument of the young and bunny sailor who perished in the war like everyone . . ."

But a pitcher thrown from a distance by an indignant colombophile

hits the man who was telling how he loved to laugh between the eyes.
He falls. The Soldier Pigeon is avenged. The paper-masked officials
crush the man's head under their heels and the young girl, who soaks
the end of her parasol in blood for a souvenir, emits a charming little
laugh. The music resumes.

The man's head is red like a too-red tomato, one eye hangs from the
end of a nerve, but in the demolished face, the living eye, the left
one, shines like a lantern over ruins.

"Take it away," says the President, and the man, lying on a
stretcher with his face hidden by a policeman's cape, leaves the Elysée
horizontally, one man behind him, another in front.

"You've got to laugh a little," he says to the sentry and the sentry
watches him go with that curdling look that the high-livers put on
before the low.

Cut out of the iron curtain of the pharmacy a star of light shines
and like the magi kings looking for infant Jesus the butcher boys, the
eiderdown salesmen and all good-hearted men contemplate the star
which tells them that the man is inside, that he isn't quite dead, that
he is probably being cared for and all wait for him to come out with
the hope of finishing him off.

They wait, and finally, on all fours because of the too-small opening in the iron curtain, the police magistrate enters the shop, the
druggist helps him up and shows him the dead man, his head sup-
ported on the baby scales.

And the magistrate wonders, and the druggist watches the magistrate wondering whether this isn't the same man who threw confetti
on the hearse for the field-marshal and who, before, put the infernal
machine on the route of the little corporal.

And then they talk about their little deals, about their children,
about their bronchial conditions; dawn comes, the curtains are pulled
at the President's place.

Outside it is spring, animals, flowers. In the Clamart woods you
hear the clamor of children playing around, it is spring, an affectionate
rumpus of the needle in the compass, the four-eyes enters the ash-
hauler and the tall dolichocephal lolls on her sofa in a silly sprawl.

The weather is warm. In love, the incendiary matches roll upon
their scratch pad, it is spring, the acne of collegians and there the
sultan's daughter and the Mandragora tamer, there the pelican's knees,
the flowers on the balconies, there the can for sprinkling water, it's the
season of birds and bees.

The sun shines for everyone; it doesn't shine in prison, it doesn't
shine for those who work in mines
those who scale fish by the ton

those who eat spoiled meat
those who manufacture hair pins
those who blow empty bottles that others will drink full
those who slice bread with their own knife
those who spend their vacations in factories
those who don't know what they are supposed to say
those who milk cows and don't drink the milk
those they don't put to sleep at the dentist's
those who spit out their lungs in subways
those who construct in cellars fountain pens with which others in the
    open air will write that things are just fine
those who have too much to say to be able to say it
those who have work
those who don't have it
those who look for it
those who don't look for it
those who carry water to horses
those who watch their dog die
those who have their daily bread more or less by the week
those who get warm in the winter in churches
those whom the sexton sends outdoors to get warm
those who stagnate
those who would like to eat to live
those who ride the rods
those who watch the Seine flowing by
those who are hired, who are fired, who are raised, who are cut, who
    are manipulated, who are pigeonholed, who are beaten to death
those from whom they take fingerprints
those whom they pull from the ranks arbitrarily and shoot
those who are made to file before the Ark
those who don't know how to behave in the whole wide world
those who have never seen the sea
those who smell like linen because they weave linen
those who don't have running water
those who are dedicated to battle gray
those who throw salt on snow for an absolutely derisory wage
those who grow old faster than others
those who don't save string
those who die of boredom on Sunday afternoon because they see
    Monday coming and Tuesday, and Wednesday, and Thursday, and
    Friday and Saturday and Sunday afternoon.

Anti-Bourgeoisie

The poem begins with a group portrait of the model citizenry. The poet ticks off the traits of its members, not by means of adjectives, but by means of carefully chosen adverbs, coined verbs and clichés which stress action and speech rather than appearance, as a film scenario does. Considering only the opening litany, where every line begins "Those who . . . ," one finds that the dinner guests are ostensibly religious ("Those who piously . . . ," "Those who believe"), patriotic ("Those who tricolor"), militaristic ("Those who dreadnought"), and accomplished, suave and orderly ("Those who sing in time, Those who can carve chicken")—the portrait, in short, of a conventional, well-bred, bourgeois company, the portrait of all that Prévert detests.

By implication, all "those" are of one kind, and the last seven lines of the opening "inventory" charge them with three cardinal prévertian crimes: cruelty, conceit, and cowardice. Those who could strew the top of the wall of China with broken bottles are cruel; those who uppercase are conceited; and those who steal eggs and are afraid to eat them are cowards.

The most grievous of those middle-class sins appears to be that of cruelty through indifference or insensitivity to human suffering. The masks, or heads, of piety, pomposity and chauvinism are the barriers between privileged classes and any perception of the misery around them. The minister of protocol is concerned with order among the spoons while suffering in the streets is ignored. In his absurd speech, the President himself seems to care more for flies, because they require the manufacture of fly swatters, than he cares for a dying child.

It becomes clearer, as the dinner unfolds, that even though Prévert associates the bourgeoisie with the great crime of insensitivity, it is the crime he condemns rather than the class to which it belongs. The implication that the two go together is obvious, but it is still only an implication, for the poet sticks to sketches and parables of a concrete nature. Up until the time of the entrance of the man's head man the poem is a string of such sketches, most of them illustrating the great sin but never slipping into a revolutionist's abstract rant.

So, again, it is the action and the character type, not the verbal tag, at which Prévert rails. This preoccupation with the thing itself, in the form of words as concrete and specific as possible, has a direct bearing on this poet's view of his own art and its effectiveness, but for now let it be noted that such poetry can hardly be labeled outright propaganda. One must recognize the unsubtle attempt to associate social classes with character traits, but it would be unjust to charge the poet with a false generalization. He simply does not ordinarily make generalizations.

Midway through the dinner, which up to that point has been a grotesque cartoon of the vices of humanity, a man "with a man's head" joins the company uninvited. He is the first of a long series of proletarian protagonists, and he crashes the party in order to tell the assembled members of the leisure class what the worker's misery is like. He seems to be a representative for all the underprivileged and overworked. (". . . I speak here for the bedridden, I monologue for longshoremen, I phonograph for the splendid dolts of Skid Row. . . .") He invites the company to visit the slums and see everyday tragedies. They ought to be amused, he adds, masking bitterness in irony, as they were amused as children by a visit to the zoo.

But the man's head man knows the guests will not follow him into the streets to view and be touched by the suffering there, so he warns them of the consequences of their indifference—revolution.

Because that head, so faintly alive, that you move under dead pasteboard . . . that head with all its wrinkles, all its trained grimaces, one day you will shake it off your trunk with a detached air and when it falls in the sawdust you will say neither yes nor no.[8]

The protagonist, after referring to the old pastime of beheading kings, makes his warning more specific, more immediate. He begins an inventory of his own, listing the targets of the hinted revolution.

And when I say, Monsieur President, Ladies and Gentlemen, the King, the Queen, the little princes, I do it to cover things generally, because you can't reasonably blame regicides who don't have a king at hand if they sometimes exercise their talents in their immediate surroundings.

Particularly among those who think that a handful of rice is enough to feed a whole Chinese family for long years.[9]

At last it dawns on the assembled company that the man is talking about people much like themselves. At last his words penetrate the diners' indifference. Feeling his charges to be more threat than warning, they grow angry and beat him almost to death. Here the masks are stripped off, figuratively if not actually, and only the cruelty, hypocrisy, and cowardice of this society remain. The man with a man's head, and a man's feeling for other men, becomes a sort of Communist Christ, who is crucified by those to whom he brought his truth.

Pro-Proletariat

To correspond with the opening inventory of phrases suggesting the qualities of the leisure class, Prévert finishes his poem with a list of the sufferings of the poor for whom the martyred man pleaded. Yet, although Prévert's attack on the dinner party, representing the worst aspects of the bourgeoisie, is openly malicious, his expression of sympathy with the workers does not stem from any stated belief in their superior virtue. The inventories of the two classes are both in a sense negative. The moneyed people are condemned for their selfish insensitivity, hypocrisy, pomposity, and cowardice. The destitute are not praised, however, in this particular poem, for the virtues which are opposites of these vices; they are merely presented as innocent victims who suffer because others are corrupt. Their real virtue, if it can be called such, is unsought martyrdom.

This final section names "those who" do not see the sun, do not eat regularly, cannot express their miseries, and find almost no joy in life. Again, although the phrase "working class" might identify generally those whom the poet is talking about, Prévert enumerates specific occupations and emotional situations, avoiding an overt, argumentative appeal and letting the examples build into a solid, unequivocal demand on our sympathies.

Thus the rich have or can do ("Those who can carve chicken, Those who know a hawk from a handsaw, Those who float and don't sink," etc.), whereas the poor have not or can not ("Those who don't know what to say, those who have never seen the sea, those who don't have running water," etc.). The wealthy and accomplished even have capitalized pronouns (Those), while the underprivileged are referred to only in small letters (those). This subtle discrimination Prévert notes ironically within the poem ("Those who uppercase"), jibing at the pomposity of official titles.

The essential power of the poem does not stem from the validity of its sociological analysis—which is certainly biased and oversimplified—but from its emotional appeal. Whether those who cut their bread with a knife are any "better" than those who put broken glass on the Great Wall of China is not really the question. The latter hurt the former, and that is the injustice; that is, simply enough, the wrong against which the whole poem protests.

The logical conclusions which this poem implies—but one must always remember they are only implied—are hardly tenable *outside the poem*. In *Dîner de têtes* those with colonial plantations and factories are greedy and do not care about the peasants under them. Therefore, the poor have justification for assassinating their overseers; they are avenging injustice. However, Prévert has invented the colonial and industrial ogres himself, and they are straw ogres, or to repeat Queval's analogy, puppets. It is fair, *within the poem*, to destroy them, for no one can reasonably claim that puppets represent accurately an entire class.

It is necessary to recognize the puppet-show quality of Prévert's work and the distortion and simplification of reality it involves, because in a few poems the puppets, which can be amusing and edifying, are abandoned. There is left only an ugly, hysterical complaint against rather vague grievances. Without caricature of character types, the poetry appears flimsy. It develops both logical and technical faults.

Before studying an example of such faults, however, one may well examine two poems which treat only one theme each by means of one specific example. *La Grasse Matinée*, best classified as a pro-proletariat poem, and *Riviera*, which belongs to the anti-bourgeois group, succeed brilliantly because they deal with individuals in unique situations without striving to imply forcefully that one class causes another's misery. *Matinée* is actually about one unemployed man, not about the proletariat, and *Riviera* records the character of a single bourgeois matron, saying little about the whole class.

MORNING FOR SLEEPING IN*

It is terrible
the little noise of a hard-boiled egg cracked on a tin counter
it is a terrible noise
when it stirs in the memory of a man who is hungry
the head of the man is terrible too
the head of a man who is hungry
when he looks at himself at six o'clock in the morning
in the window of a big store
a head the color of dust
it isn't however his head that he looks at
in the display window of Potin's place
he doesn't give a goddamn for his head
the man
he doesn't think about it
he dreams
he imagines another head
a head of veal for example
with a vinegar sauce
or a head of anything whatever which can be eaten
and he moves his jaw softly
softly
and he grits his teeth softly
because the world makes fun of him
he can't do anything against this world
and he counts on his fingers one two three
one two three
that makes three days without eating
and it's been no use repeating for three days
This can't last
it lasts
three days
three nights
without eating
and behind these display windows
these *pâtés* these bottles these jams
dead fish protected by cans
cans protected by windows
windows protected by cops
cops protected by fear
so many barricades for six pitiful sardines

* Original French text of this translation appears on page 141.

"Pro" and "Anti" Themes

A little further on the cafe
coffee with cream and hot rolls
The man sways
and inside his head
a fog of words
a fog of words
sardines to eat
hard-boiled egg coffee with cream
coffee laced with rum
coffee with cream
coffee with cream
coffee with crime laced with blood! . . .
A man highly esteemed in his neighborhood
had his throat cut in broad daylight
the killer the bum stole a sum
of two francs
or a coffee with rum
zero francs seventy
two buttered rolls
and twenty-five centimes for the waiter's tip.

It is terrible
the little noise of a hard-boiled egg cracked on a tin counter
it is a terrible noise
when it stirs in the memory of a man who is hungry.

RIVIERA*

Seated in a long reclining chair
a lady with a faded tongue
a long lady
longer than her long chair
and no longer young
takes her ease
they probably told her that the sea was there
so she looks at it
she doesn't see it though
and presidents pass by and bow very low
it's baroness Crin
queen of the dental cavity
her husband is baron Crin

* Original French text of this translation appears on page 143.

king of rabbit fertilizer
and at her large feet all are in their little shoes
and they pass before her and bow very low
from time to time
she throws them an old toothpick
they suck it, ecstatic,
continuing their walk
their new shoes crack and their old bones too
and from the villas comes a pallid music
a music thin, sharp
and certain
like the cries of a newborn child too long neglected
it's our sons
it's our sons say the presidents
and they nod their heads gently and proudly
and their little prodigies
desperately
throw their piano pieces in one another's faces
the baroness lends an ear
this music pleases her
but her ear falls
like an old shingle from a roof
she looks down
and she doesn't see it
but merely notices it
and takes it
quite good-naturedly
for a dead leaf brought by the wind
it is then that the children
stop their mournful din
which the baroness no longer heard anyway
except with an ear distracted
and uneven
then surges up abruptly
and frolics in her poor head
in utter liberty
every puerile naughty outmoded air
of her memory, worn uneasy, and plucked bare
and as she searches vainly
to pass the time
which menaces her and spies on her
for a nice regret very sad and very sentimental
which could make her laugh until tears came

> or even merely weep
> she finds only an indecent incongruous memory
> the image of an old lady seated stark naked
> on a camel's hump
> while naughtily knitting a guano omelet.

Riviera introduces a sort of Lady Prufrock, a rich, old capitalist dowager who seems to have lost interest in everything. She has carried one of the prévertian vices, insensitivity, to such a point that the emptiness it creates in her life shuts out all perception. She even fails to notice her own aged ear when it drops off and "falls like an old roof tile," though finally she sees it on the ground and mistakes it for a dead leaf ("feuille" can mean both "leaf" and "ear" in French. Prévert deliberately plays on this confusion). Searching, under the influence of the thin, resentful piano-lesson music of children, for a sentimental memory, she finds only a grotesque daymare, the image of a naked old lady on a camel knitting a guano omelet. Here is the crude, bold tempera of one person's spiritual decay; Prufrock is a subtle miniature of the same.

La Grasse Matinée argues the case of a man who murders for a meal by trying to make the reader sense the torturing, dizzying pangs of starvation that can drive one to crime. For Prévert, the law of hunger, a natural law of the body, prevails over man-made laws when the two conflict. He tries to make the reader feel the power of the hunger law—which establishes its legitimacy—in the gnawing rhythm early in the poem, which quickens to a frenzy of free-association at the end, and in the contrast between tantalizing gustatory images and flat, bare statements of pain. Given the terrible, "lawless" power generated by the hunger drive, one understands the danger and injustice of thwarting it by means of windows and policemen. It would be too much to say that Prévert tries to justify murder in the name of hunger; however, he certainly bids for our sympathy toward the criminal, who, though turned into an animal by circumstances, still tipped the waiter generously with the dead man's money. Society had not been so kind to him.

Le Retour au pays is another poem wherein Prévert attempts to show how crime arises naturally in an oppressive environment.

COMING HOME*

This man from Brittany came back to his native land
After having pulled a number of jobs
He takes a walk by the factories at Douarnenez
He doesn't recognize anybody
Nobody recognizes him
He's sad.
He goes into a hot-dog stand to eat some hot dogs
But he can't eat any
Something keeps them from going down
He pays
He goes out
He lights a cigarette
But he can't smoke it.
There is something
Something in his head yet
Something wrong
He gets sadder and sadder
And suddenly he begins to remember:
Someone told him when he was little
"You'll end up on the gallows"
And for years
He hasn't dared do anything ever
Not even cross the street
Not even take a trip by sea
Nothing absolutely nothing.
He remembers.
The one who predicted it all was uncle Sizzloff
Uncle Sizzloff who brought bad luck to everybody
The crumb!
And the man from Brittany thinks of his sister
Who works at Vaugirard
Of his brother killed in the war
Thinks of all the things he has seen
All the things he has done.
Sadness presses in on him
He tries again
To light a cigarette
But he doesn't feel like smoking
Then he decides to go see uncle Sizzloff.
He goes

* Original French text of this translation appears on page 144.

> He opens the door
> His uncle doesn't recognize him
> But he recognizes him
> And says:
> "Hello uncle Sizzloff"
> And then he wrings his neck.
> And he ends up on the gallows at Quimper
> After having eaten a dozen hot dogs
> And smoked a cigarette.

Both the hungry man in *Matinée* and the lonely man in *Retour* are victims of circumstance; their environment determines their fate. *Retour* concerns a man who has been inhibited all his life by the dicta and predictions of his elders. Unable to enjoy life, fearful under the yoke of a vindictive prophecy, the man goes back home and strangles his relative out of frustration and, perhaps, a mournful sense of poetic justice. He dies on the gallows, of course, to fulfill his fate, but not before having enjoyed a meal and a smoke for the first time.

This view of man trapped and directed toward his destiny by a previous generation that has ossified into conservatism is neatly expressed in the little poem *Le Droit Chemin* ("The Right Way"):

> For each kilometer
> each year
> old men with dullard's brows
> point out to children the road
> with a gesture in reinforced concrete.
>
> A chaque kilomètre
> chaque année
> des vieillards au front borné
> indiquent aux enfants la route
> d'un geste de ciment armé.[10]

The man from Brittany was punished for not taking that road, but he got his revenge by sideswiping one of the stupid old men with concrete arms.

Revolt

The poet often suggests that the more of these dotards one bowls over the better, since conventional, respected authority always interferes with the expression of man's natural, free spirit.

> When you drew straws
> it was always the cabin boy who was served up
> but the time of happy shipwrecks is past
> when admirals fall into the sea
> don't count on us to throw them a life preserver
> unless it's made of stone. . . .

> Quand vous tiriez à la courte paille
> c'était toujours le mousse qu'on bouffait
> mais le temps des joyeux naufrages est passé
> lorsque les amiraux tomberont à la mer
> ne comptez pas sur nous pour leur jeter la bouée
> à moins qu'elle ne soit en pierre. . . .[11]

Not always does the idea of revolt remain merely a suggestion. In many poems Prévert calls for blood. Some critics seem oddly chary of recognizing this shouting for the heads to roll, though it appears in plenty of places and in a loud, clear voice. Queval at first denies that Prévert can qualify as an anarchist.

No, it is not a matter of anarchy. Prévert, I believe, has nowhere written the word "anarchy"; it is not a question of bomb-throwing; neither is it in any way a question of shooting at the piano player.[12]

The fact that Prévert has never written the word "anarchy" may be of no significance at all; there are probably many bomb-throwers who do not go about openly avowing their profession. In *Dîner de têtes*, however, the man's head man recommends a little gun cotton in the ears of monarchs, and there is no getting around the bloodthirsty implication of that prescription.

Queval later remarks this militant, revolutionary quality of Prévert's anti-bourgeois poetry.

For this poetry is not that of resignation, but that of combat. . . . To what degree Prévert's poetry is militant need not be repeated.[13]

This contradiction in Queval's commentary, which occurs also to a certain extent in the criticism of George Bataille and Albert Gaudin, stems partly from a contradiction in Prévert. When, occasionally, Prévert sheds his role of satiric dramatist and attacks with bombastic propaganda, the result is a poetry full of unsound assumptions, exaggerated emotionalism, and gross faults of taste. The poem *Le Paysage changeur* (*Paroles*, p. 106), for example, contains this scattergun tirade against capitalism:

> the countryside without air without light without laughter
>   or seasons
> the frozen countryside of the workers' cities frozen in
>   midsummer as in the heart of winter
> the burnt-out countryside
> the countryside without anything
>
> .   .   .   .
>
> On this countryside a star sometimes shines
> a single one
> the false sun
> the pallid sun
> the setting sun
> the dog sun of capital
>
> .   .   .   .
>
> the revolting sun of the sun king
> the sun over Austerlitz
> the sun over Verdun
> the fetishist sun
> the sun tricolor and colorless
> disastrous astral body
> star of rats
> star of slaughter
> star of bastardliness
> the dead sun.
>
> le paysage sans air sans lumière sans rires ni saisons
> le paysage glacé des cités ouvrières glacées en plein été
>   comme au coeur de l'hiver
> le paysage éteint
> le paysage sans rien
>
> .   .   .   .

Sur ce paysage parfois un astre luit
un seul
le faux soleil
le soleil blème
le soleil couché
le soleil chien du capital
. . . .

le dégôutant soleil du roi soleil
le soleil d'Austerlitz
le soleil de Verdun
le soleil fétiche
le soleil tricolor et incolore
l'astre des désastres
l'astre de la vacherie
l'astre de la tuerie
l'astre de la connerie
le soleil mort.

Besides the rank anthropomorphism of the sun and countryside "symbols," and the questionable worth of such wordplay as "astre des désastres," the poet also destroys his paper villain, capitalism, with too easy a blow. A real sun, Prévert writes, will replace the false one when the workers revolt: "the true hard red sun of revolution." If there is opposition on the part of capitalistic interests, the proletariat will destroy them: "One last time capital will try to keep them from laughing/they will kill it." Such a vision of future class struggle and its outcome, pretending to the apocalyptic, does not coincide very well with one of the statements of the man's head man: "I have no crystal ball, I have no tea leaves. I haven't the cotton-batting beard of those who make prophecies." But Prévert brings out a false beard from time to time, and it is then, when he forgets himself and puts on the whiskers of a political prophet, that he loses the charm and piquancy of the puppet-show director.

One Prévert paradox, involving his ambivalent attitude toward violence, now becomes clear. In identifying the "false sun" of capital with the suns over Austerlitz and Verdun, Prévert again associates capitalism and war. Detesting war, Prévert then detests capitalism; it follows—and too easily here—that to destroy

war one need only destroy capitalism. And the only way to kill
capitalism—let us be as specific as Prévert—is to kill capitalists.
Hence this inevitable paradox: though constantly throughout his
work Prévert expresses a hatred for war, he nevertheless at times
cries out clearly for revolt—for bloodshed if necessary—to cure
the ills of a capitalistic order.[14] This paradox renders unsound
and unconvincing some of Prévert's work; and poems containing
such bald inconsistencies often lack original, powerful imagery.
Certainly the attack in *Paysage* has little of the sting so notable
in *Dîner de têtes*.

Anti-Church

The two largest ogres in Prévert's puppet retinue are the
bourgeoisie and the Church. Against them he has released his
longest, heaviest barrage; the two poems *Dîner de têtes* and *La
Crosse en l'air* make up about one-fourth of the entire first collection, *Paroles*. *La Crosse en l'air* is a savage diatribe against
the Catholic Church. It is both more bitter and more specific
than *Dîner*. The man's head man snipes at cardboard masks, but
his counterpart in *La Crosse*, the night watchman, aims his insults and obscenities directly at the Pope. And they are insults
and obscenities of unmistakably greater rancor.

The night watchman, whom we can take as the proletarian in
this poem, is an utter atheist. In his interview with the Pope he
makes this plain.

> and the other confidentially in his ear
> the other begins bellowing
> Hello hello Holy Father you hear me
> atheist
> A as in absolutely atheist
> T as in totally atheist
> H as in hermetically atheist
> E short e as in extraordinarily atheist
> IST as in incorrigibly surely thoroughly atheist
>
> et l'autre dans le tuyau de son oreille
> l'autre se met à gueuler
> Allô allô Saint-Père vous m'entendez
> athée

A comme absolument athée
T comme totalement athée
H comme hermétiquement athée
É accent aigu comme étonnamment athée
E comme entièrement athée[15]

Without God, the entire edifice of the Church becomes an absurd and disgusting sham; its terminology, icons, and employees are worthy only of spiteful ridicule. Prévert does more than mock, however; he insults with brutal directness. The Pope's person, for example, is described thus:

> that big head with all the marks
> of professional deformity
> dignity unction extreme unction
>   cruelty slyness hypocrisy
> and all those poses
> all those lugubrious and somber buffooneries.

> cette grande tête avec toutes les marques
> de la déformation professionnelle
> la dignité l'onction l'extrême-onction
>   la cruauté la roublardise la papelardise
> et tous ces simulacres
> toutes ces mornes et sérieuses pitreries[16]

As for the sacredness of titles, "one must," says Prévert, "call things by their names." But the nomenclature of the Church, he goes on to imply, deceives by attaching new, gilded tags to things not sacred at all.

> a flower is a flower
> but a pope what's that
> a hideous old man

> une fleur c'est une fleur
> mais un pape qu'est-ce que c'est
> un affreux vieillard[17]

The poet's technique of ridicule often depends on an assumption of the hollowness of words. He satirizes the sacred concepts of Christianity by discussing them in everyday jargon, just as one may satirize the everyday by describing it in biblical language. There are times when Prévert seems to be doing both. In *Souvenirs de famille* (*Paroles*, 31) for example, the crucifixion is described in trade jargon, a metaphor which thus relates Christianity and commercialism.

> Comfortably installed on his flagship cloud, God the father, of the firm God father son Holy Ghost and Co., heaves an immense sigh of satisfaction, immediately two or three little employee clouds burst forth obsequiously and God the father cries: "Let me be praised, my holy enterprise be blessed; with my beloved son on the cross, my firm is launched!"

> Confortablement installé sur son nuage amiral, Dieu le père, de la maison Dieu père fils Saint-Esprit et Cie, pousse un immense soupir de satisfaction, aussitôt deux ou trois petits nuages subalternes éclatent avec obséquiosité et Dieu père s'écrie: "Que je sois loué que ma sainte raison sociale soit bénie, mon fils bien-aimé à la croix, ma maison est lancée!"[18]

Note that in the original the rhyme, infantile and repetitious as an advertising slogan, adds to the effect of cheapening the sacred.

There are a number of parallels between Prévert's attack on organized religion and his attitude toward the bourgeoisie. One of the more obvious of these is the poet's inflexible hostility toward the official representatives of both groups.

> Prévert's anti-clericalism is of the most unwavering, most scorching, most explosive sort. It is also the most intransigent. No salvation in his eyes for the priests of the Catholic Church.[19]

Queval's phrase "also, naturally, the most intransigent" betrays how commonly such intolerant views appear in Prévert.

Also, much as Prévert seems to link the greed of capitalists with the misery of the proletariat, paying not the slightest heed to any theorist's evidence to the contrary, he refuses to see anything in Catholicism but an instrument to twist and suffocate the free, natural spirit of man—the source of his happiness. Once one tangles with an angel, as in *Le Combat avec l'ange*, one can never make love again. And that, as far as this poet is concerned, makes angels into devils. (Blake, of course, makes this inversion explicit; and Prévert has written a poem in praise of Blake—*Noces et banquets*, in *Paroles*, 275.) Theologians may argue most intelligently until kingdom come, but his position of the heart taken, Prévert never budges.

The powers of abstract reason will not dislodge Jacques Prévert from the position of fearless and stubborn sniper which he occupies in the atheist camp. His is not one of those intelligences, wide-ranging perhaps, but seemingly localized in the cerebral lobes, uneasy, open to influences, and, like weather-cocks, shifting with every wind. On the contrary, we have to do here with an organic intelligence, in André Malraux's apt phrase.[20]

One of the secrets of the effectiveness of this "organic intelligence," as has already been mentioned, involves steering clear of dialectic and limiting oneself to the concrete. Prévert's most telling attacks on the social order are launched upon a single character in a single incident. Similarly, the poet concentrates on the trappings of Christianity rather than on its metaphysics. He has almost a phobia against formal arguments, which he can ridicule artfully because he assigns no validity to them. Men may commit stupidities in the name of ideas, but Prévert blames the individual, not his limbless belief. So, just as one cannot accuse this poetry of being mere propaganda, he must also recognize that Prévert's hostility to religion operates on the personal, not on a dialectical level.

Even the critics' hesitancy in recognizing the pungency of Prévert's revolutionary idiom has its parallel here. Queval insists that there is no hate behind the insults thrown at the Church.

Hate—in Prévert's work it is not to be found, and his indignation sometimes makes one think of Don Quixote demolishing Master Pedro's marionettes. It is not with hate that one upsets into the pit the mayor, the mother-in-law, the game-keeper.[21]

Again the critic resorts to the puppet-show figure. But, though it is true Prévert can create clerics, as well as bourgeois, who are made of straw, there remains his personal attack on the papacy. Nor is it now true that Prévert has never written the word "hate," as Bataille was able to claim in 1946. *Spectacle* (1951) contains at the end of the first poem the pun "Âme Haine." There is no reason to try so hard to avoid uncovering another paradox. Professing fraternal love for the common people, Prévert still reveals flashes of what one may well call hatred for the Catholic clergy.

Instead of hate, Queval speaks of horror and detestation, which he thinks are also Prévert's sentiments toward the bourgeoisie.

Let us not say hate; let us say horror. This feeling that Prévert has for matters of religion is directed toward the influence they exert on men among themselves, as it appears to him. He sees a Catholic social philosophy now and for some time of a distinctly pharisaical cast. . . . A Christianity become the bulwark and alibi of the bourgeois order is at the vital center of all the poet detests with his whole heart.[22]

Recognizing the relationship—Prévert would call it the conspiracy—between the bourgeoisie and the Church, one can foresee a corresponding correlation of atheism and the proletariat. The night watchman, outspoken atheist protagonist of *La Crosse,* joins the man's head man as a mouthpiece of the working class, by reason of his occupation and by reason of his blunt, common-sense view of the world. There is even an inventory of the watchman's friends, encountered on the road to the Vatican, which recalls the groups which the man's head man represented.

. . . his ironworker comrades who fabricate houses at the Port of Champerret for his cement-worker comrades . . . his gutter-sweeping comrades . . . overworked comrades . . . fishermen comrades of Douarnenez . . . exploited comrades . . . comrades from the T.C.R.P. . . . underpaid comrades . . . latrine-cleaning comrades . . . humiliated comrades . . . Chinese comrades from the rice paddies of China . . . starved comrades. . . .

. . . ses camarades charpentiers en fer qui fabriquent les maisons de la porte Champerret pour ses camarades cimentiers . . . ses camarades égoutiers . . . camarades surmenés . . . camarades pêcheurs de Douarnenez . . . camarades exploités . . . camarades de la T.C.R.P.

[51]

... camarades mal payés ... camarades vidangeurs ... camarades humiliés ... camarades chinois des rizières de Chine ... camarades affamés. ...[23]

Once again the poor, the hungry, the beaten and the humiliated march by, a mute, menacing reproach to the finery of churchman and merchant.

CHAPTER 2

The Ogre Gallery and the House of Love

The prévertian world begins to take shape; on one side are "Those" who have and worship false idols, on the other are those who have not and believe in themselves. The cast will be complete with the addition of military men and intellectuals to the ranks of the bad guys, and children, beautiful women, and birds to the ranks of the good. These additions do not pair off into neat antipodes, however, as do the bourgeoisie and the proletariat. Prévert regards with affection a number of diverse character types who have in common only the sentiment of love and the will to freedom, rather than occupations which can serve as class symbols. Against religion, for example, one would have to mention both the love of man for woman and the child's love of freedom. And against the regimentation of militarism one can pose whatever is free and natural: the rebellious child, the uninhibited man and woman, the hobo.

Although a number of long poems would better illustrate the intensity of Prévert's antipathy to war, the short one *Familiale* deserves attention here because it links war to the bourgeoisie.

FAMILY FEELING*

The mother knits
The son wages war
She finds this quite natural the mother
And the father what does the father do?
He is busy in business
His wife does her knitting
His son war

* Original French text of this translation appears on page 146.

He business
He finds this quite natural the father
And the son the son
What does he find the son?
He finds nothing absolutely nothing the son
The son his mother does her knitting his father business he war
When he finishes the war
He will be busy in business with his father
The war goes on the mother goes on she knits
The father goes on he is busy in business
The son is killed he goes on no more
The father and the mother go to the graveyard
They find that quite natural the father and mother
Life goes on life with knitting war business
Business war knitting war
Business business business
Life with the graveyard.

War, knitting, and business—occupations not usually grouped as family activities—belong together in Prévert's view of the world. Knitting is the pastime of the conventional homemaker, business the very breath of life for the middle-class man, and war the legacy of blind conventionality and avarice—that is the skeleton of relationships underlying the poem. With a repetitive rhyme scheme reinforcing the theme of mechanical, monotonous adherence to convention, the poem strongly hints at a causal connection between families in an inflexible routine of menial chores and penny-squeezing, and the wars which the sons of those families must fight. The horror of this routine is that even the deaths of war are accepted as something as natural as knitting by the fireside.

The poem *Barbara*, simple, straightforward and lyrical, is one of Prévert's finest war poems. The bitter protest involves no direct attack on social classes or economic conditions: it is based on the simple grounds that war destroyed the happiness of a young girl walking in the rain to meet her lover. Perhaps those are the best grounds. Certainly Prévert's technique of dramatizing the tragedy of war or poverty by means of ordinary, yet individual characters apparently photographed at random, is more successful artistically than his didactic comments, no matter how lucid and clever, on the entire human pageant. It is a simple fact that one almost always grieves more for the Barbaras of the world than for a whole impersonal army.

BARBARA*

Remember Barbara
It rained endlessly on Brest that day
And you walked smiling
Blooming enraptured streaming
In the rain
Remember Barbara
It rained endlessly on Brest
And I ran across you on the Rue de Siam
You smiled
And me I did the same
Remember Barbara
You whom I didn't know
You who didn't know me
Remember though
Remember that day even so
Don't forget
A man was taking shelter under a porch
And he cried out your name
Barbara
And you ran in the rain toward him
Streaming enraptured blossoming
And you threw yourself in his arms
Remember that Barbara
And don't be angry if I speak so intimately
I talk that way to all those I love
Even if I've seen them one time only
I say that to all those who love
Even if I don't know them yet
Remember Barbara
Don't forget
That wise and happy rain
On your happy face
On that happy town
That rain on the sea

* Original French text of this translation appears on page 146.

On the arsenal
On the Oessant scow
Oh Barbara
What a screwed up war
What has become of you now
Under that rain of iron
Of iron of steel of gore
And the one who held you in his arms
Lovingly
Is he dead missing or living still
Oh Barbara
It rains endlessly on Brest
As it rained before
But it's no longer the same everything is gutted
It is a rain of grief terrible and desolate
It isn't even the storm anymore
Of iron of steel of gore
Quite simply some clouds
Which die like dogs
Dogs which vanish
Into the flow of water on Brest
And go to rot far away
Far very far away from Brest
Of which there is nothing left.

This poem also brings one to a clearer realization of the nature of the conflict, as Prévert sees it, between church and state, and the individual. It is a conflict stemming from the supposed attempt of religious, social, or political institutions to restrict or destroy the natural appetites of man. As windows and cops stood between the hungry man and the sardines, a bombing separated Barbara and her lover. Windows, cops, bombs—the conventional machinery of society to "protect" the property and lives of its members—end by spoiling the happiness in these lives. This idea appears again and again in the poetry of Prévert, who wishes to supplant the laws of institutions with the unwritten law of free, natural expression of one's will. "The natural order supplants the supernatural; and love, religion. . . ."[24]

A number of poems show that freedom is the principle unifying all the values Prévert upholds, particularly in the matter of love. The kind of love Prévert endorses could be called free love in its usual sense and also "free" love in the sense that no restrictions ought to be imposed by either party in such relationships. The subject is handled with telling irony in the little poem *Pour toi mon amour.*

FOR YOU MY LOVE*

I went to the market for birds
And I bought some birds
For you
my love
I went to the market for flowers
And I bought some flowers
For you
my love
I went to the market for iron
And I bought some chains
Some heavy chains
For you
my love
And next I went to the market for slaves
And I looked for you
But I didn't find you
my love.

The lover ought not to have gone hopefully to the slave market, for he will never find his "beloved" there. In Prévert's ideal world one cannot capture another human being—people bind themselves to one another voluntarily. Similarly, in *Il a tourné autour de moi* (*Spectacle*, 193) the boy who asks for no token of love is the one who gets the girl.

Many of the poet's metaphors stress the natural, spontaneous character of free love. Many lines, for example, liken woman to a lush fruit or to the sun,[25] suggesting that she too is one of the bounties of nature meant to be taken with unthinking gusto.

* Original French text of this translation appears on page 148.

ALICANTE*

An orange on the table
Your dress on the carpet
And you in my bed
Sweet present of the present
Cool of the evening
Warmth of my being.

Such uncomplicated, open sensuality is not to be confused with a covetous lust that drives one to try to enslave another. In fact Prévert everywhere implies that freedom—in the largest sense of the word—is a precondition for true passion and that only the freely given "present of the present" is completely natural, uncorrupted.

Birdland

The poet's favorite emblem of nature is the bird—the bird, surely, because birds symbolize freedom.[26] And freedom, complete freedom, is the "natural order"—really a sort of disorder—with which the poet would supplant man's political, religious, and social systems. In *La Crosse* the poet elects the bird, the child and the worker to fight against the tyranny of religion. A bird attacks the Pope, figurehead of religious authority, with the wholehearted consent of the night watchman. Prévert calls this bird the "bird of youth," thus identifying the child too with the natural will to freedom.

It's the bird of youth
the bird who breaks into volleys of laughter
... and there goes the pope uttering a long cry
of distress, plunging down and
rolling on the ground and lying in critical condition and
getting up again howling
he received a volley of laughter in the eye
and keeping up his howling he circles around
his armchair running
pursued by the scornful bird

* Original French text of this translation appears on page 148.

the bird that laughs like a child
Go on let him alone says the watchman to the bird
let him alone he's an old man
save yourself . . . get out of here . . .

c'est l'oiseau de la jeunesse
l'oiseau qui rit aux éclats
. . . et voilà le pape qui pousse un long cri
de détresse et qui pique une tête et qui
roule à terre et qui pique une crise et qui
se relève en hurlant
il a reçu un éclat de rire dans l'oeil
et continuant son hurlement il tourne autour
de son fauteuil en courant
poursuivi par l'oiseau moqueur
l'oiseau qui rit comme un enfant
Allez laisse
dit le veilleur à l'oiseau
laisse c'est un vieux
sauve-toi . . . va-t'en . . .[27]

One sees that this time Prévert lends positive qualities to his everyman from the working class. The watchman is not merely a sufferer like the hungry man. Here, and later when he cares for the wounded bird, the watchman shows his kindness, generosity and, more important, his mercy. Already, in insulting Mussolini and the Pope, he has shown courage. Courage, candor, kindness, and generous sympathy for *les petites gens*—these are the exact antitheses of the sins associated with the moneyed class. So, too, the freedom of the bird and the joyous sensuality of childhood stand opposed to the austere discipline and gloom of the Church.

Another of Prévert's *bêtes noires*, the army, also suffers defeat when it runs afoul of a bird. The bird in *Quartier libre* replaces an army cap, representing obeisance to an oppressive authority, and squelches an officer's demand for a salute.

FREE SECTOR*

I put my army cap in the cage
and I went out with the bird on my head
So
we aren't saluting anymore
demanded the commander
No
we aren't saluting anymore
replied the bird
Oh well
excuse me I thought we saluted
said the commander
You're quite excused anybody can make a mistake
said the bird.

When men, like the bird, escape from the cage of church, state, and society, there can be no more saluting, genuflecting, or back-slapping, gestures which, Prévert thinks, cramp the soul. These postures of sycophants, cowards, and hypocrites the poet would renounce in favor of the gestures of freedom and love: the comrade's handshake, the lover's caress, the child playing, and the bird in the wind.

Anti-Intellectualism

The last character type in Prévert's gallery of ogres is the intellectual, the philosopher or the musty scholar niggling over nuances of a dead idea. If left to himself, the intellectual, living in his "mental world," will expend his life erecting a self-glorifying monument of theories. It is clearly said in the poem *Il ne faut pas.* . . . Antagonistic to all traditional forms and methods of knowledge, because they cast a screen of words between man and the joy and suffering of experiencing reality, Prévert recommends that the ingrown, egocentric intellectual be watched like an idiot child.

* Original French text of this translation appears on page 149.

ONE MUSTN'T*

One mustn't let intellectuals play with matches
Because gentlemen when one leaves it alone
The mental world gen-n-ntlemen
Is not at all brilliant
And as soon as it is alone
Works arbitrarily
Erecting for itself
And generously self-styled in honor of the workers
of the development
An auto-monument
Let us repeat gen-n-n-ntlemen
When one leaves it alone
The mental world
Will lie
Monumentally.

In this poet's unique world, of course, children and washer-women are wiser in their common sense than are cultured, well-schooled adults with their degrees. Those who work solely with their minds Prévert treats as ridiculous figures, contrasting them with his heroes, who are those who work with their hands or those who do not work at all. Though he bears little resemblance otherwise to Baudelaire, Prévert too has an evil flower—thought.

Man
You looked at the saddest, most mournful of all the
    flowers on earth
And as for the other flowers you gave it a name
You called it Thought.

Homme
Tu as regardé la plus triste la plus morne de toutes
    les fleurs de la terre
Et comme aux autres fleurs tu lui as donné un nom
Tu l'as appelée Pensée.[28]

* Original French text of this translation appears on page 149.

This evil flower, very gloomy alongside a real one, can be contrasted with the sunflower, both the plant and the girl, in the poem of that name. The flower of thought brings sadness, sickness, introversion, and bitterness,

> The dirty spindly little flower
> the sick flower
> the bitter flower
> the forever faded flower . . .

> La sale maigre petite fleur
> La fleur malade
> La fleur aigre
> La fleur toujours fanée . . .[29]

while women, flowers and the sun mean light, laughter, and love untainted by obfuscating and stultifying abstractions.

Philosophy, or devotion to rigorous, logical inquiry, results in a meaningless round, an agonizing querulousness. Thus the woman sings of the philosopher in *La Tour*:

> But he grows afraid
> To escape from his thought
> which makes him afraid
> He engulfs himself in the gulf
> Then
> to escape from this gulf
> He engulfs himself in his thought . . .

> Mais il prend peur
> Pour échapper à sa pensée
> Qui lui fait peur
> Il s'engouffre lui-même dans le gouffre
> Puis
> Pour échapper à ce gouffre
> Il s'engouffre dans sa pensée . . .[30]

Eventually the intellectual in his ivory tower, no matter how secluded, ruins not only his own taste for life but the happiness of others. The logical place for this point of friction is of course the school, where the discipline of academicians collides with the rebellious will to freedom of the child.

Enfants Terribles

Prévert, of course, is always on the side of the dunce, the day-dreamer, the "goof-off." He has written a number of poems expressing sympathy with their temperament, and one critic notes that the poet prefers children to adults.

Prévert loves childhood, more now probably than he loved it when he was a child. It is the world of adults, musty and ugly, which has given him the desire to regain the fountainhead of poetry, of life.[31]

But there are naturally different kinds of children just as there are different kinds of adults. Besides the heroes of *Le Cancre* (*Paroles*, 75), *Page d'écriture* (cited below), and *L'Enseignement libre* (*Spectacle*, 207), which dwell on the purity and vitality of the joys of uncivilized childhood, Prévert has his "demonic" child, already spoiled by society. Such poems as *En famille* (*Spectacle*, 123) and *L'Enfant abandonné* (*Spectacle*, 133) attack the normal family and social ties as corrupters of true, individual happiness; they satirize the little old children who have already assumed their pose and mask. One recalls too the little girl at the *Dinner of Heads* who gave grass to her rabbits and her rabbits to cobras.

Still, more than any other aspect of his work, Prévert's attitude toward the child and the child's imaginative temperament seems to earn him the title of romantic. Fay has said that the love poems are not romantic, and the pieces dealing with class conflict appear to be as allegorical as a puppet show or as factual as photographs. But the poems about children and their harmonic sympathy with nature are at least distantly related to the old notion of a superior poetry springing from primitive peoples or from the brilliant, sensual experience of childhood. Prévert's aversion to learning was preceded by Wordsworth's:

> Books! 'tis a dull and endless strife:
> Come, hear the woodland linnet,
> How sweet his music! on my life,
> There's more of wisdom in it.[32]

And Wordsworth's alternative to books—the wild bird—is also Prévert's alternative in the following poem:

NOTEBOOK LEAF*

Two and two are four
four and four eight
eight and eight make sixteen . . .
Repeat! says the teacher
Two and two are four
four and four eight
eight and eight make sixteen.
But there goes the lyre-bird
passing through the sky
the child sees him
the child hears him
the child calls him:
Save me
play with me
bird!
Then the bird descends
and plays with the child
Two and two are four . . .
Repeat! says the teacher
and the child plays
the bird plays with him
Four and four are eight
eight and eight make sixteen
and sixteen and sixteen, what does that make?
Sixteen and sixteen they don't make anything
and especially not thirty-two
anyway
and they go off.
And the child has hidden the bird
in his desk
and all the children
hear his song
and all the children
hear the music
and eight and eight in their turn go away
and four and four and two and two
in their turn run off
and one and one make neither it nor two
one and one go away just the same.
And the lyre-bird plays

* Original French text of this translation appears on page 150.

and the child sings
and the professor shouts:
Whenever you're through acting like a fool!
But all the other children
listen to the music
and the classroom walls
collapse quietly.
And the windows become sand again
the ink becomes water
the desks become trees
the chalk becomes cliff
the pen-holder becomes a bird.

CHAPTER 3

A Poetry of Anti-Poetry

One faces here what is probably the greatest of Prévert's paradoxes, the one upon which his whole approach to his art may be based. For the worker, the bird, the dunce, and the lover, words are superfluous. All of them rebel against the verbal strictures of home, Church, state, and school. The process of education tries to abstract and classify, but if one has freedom and can love, abstraction and classification are a waste of time. Therefore the dunce in *Le Cancre* erases all the names and dates, figures and mottoes, words and traps. One cannot substitute words and numbers for reality, and the attempt destroys the best in it. In the poem *Page d'écriture* sixteen and sixteen do not "make" anything—especially not thirty-two. Realizing this principle, one sees everything return to its natural state. Glass becomes sand, pencil boxes return to trees, and chalk reverts to cliff stone. They always were a part of nature; a man-made name cannot change that.

Distrusting the intellect, Prévert finally begins to question the value of its very substance—the word. One names a flower, the poet says in *La Crosse*, and one knows what it is, but one names an old man a Pope in order to trick people into thinking the old man is something more than that. And supposing one does know what "flower" means, the word is still but a word, a phantom of the brain.

Thus, although childhood may be the source of poetry, as Brindeau says, it is also very nearly its grave. In one of Prévert's love poems, *Dans ma maison*, a man finds himself alone in a strange house, waiting for a girl whom he does not yet know. At first, he amuses himself with fantastic daydreams and games with his feet which "keep one company" and without which "one can't dance." There is here all the charm of a child's idle play. But then, puzzled by the simile "gai comme un pinson," the prospective lover suddenly confronts the question of language itself, his way of expressing his love. He becomes aware of the dissociation of the word and the thing, which is the state of the world for the child as he is learning his language. And, as the man begins to view his feet in a new light, he begins also to question the whole order of language as man establishes it, and this attitude too is like the child's insistent "why?"

In My House*

Into my house you will come
Anyway it isn't my house
I don't know whose house it is
I just walked in one day
And didn't find anyone
Only red pimentos hung on the white wall
I stayed a long time in that house
No one came at all
But every day and every day
I waited there for you

I didn't do anything
That is nothing very serious
Sometimes in the morning
I bawled like an animal
I brayed like a jackass
With all my strength
And I enjoyed that
And then I played with my feet
They're very intelligent the feet
They take you very far
When you want to go very far
And when you don't want to go out
They stay there and keep you company
And whenever there is music they dance

* Original French text of this translation appears on page 151.

One can't dance without them
Got to be stupid as a man so often is
To say things as stupid
As stupid as his feet happy as a lark
The lark is not happy
He is only happy when he is happy
And sad when he is sad or neither happy nor sad
Does anyone know what a lark is
Besides he isn't really named like that
Man is the one who named the bird that way
Lark lark lark lark

How curious it is with names
Martin Hugo Victor being his first name
Bonaparte Napoleon being his first name
Why like that and not like that
A band of bonapartes goes on a desert journey
The emperor calls himself Dromedary
He has a chest of horses and a race drawer
In the distance gallops a man who has but three first names
He is called Tim-Tam-Tom and has no surname
A little further on there is no matter who
And much further on there is no matter what
And then what is all that good for

Into my house you will come
I think of other things but I think only of that
And when you have come into my house
You will take off all your clothes
And you will poise erect and naked with your red mouth
Like the red pimentos hanging on the white wall
And then you will lie down and I will lie beside you
So then
Into my house which is not my house you will come.

A Theory of Anti-Poetry

Prévert is not one of those poets who writes poems about poetry, so there is no definite statement of his artistic creed. There are, however, many poems on the art of painting, which has in this century been closely associated with poetry; and it is possible to gain some understanding of Prévert's esthetics from a study of these poems. *Pour faire le portrait d'un oiseau* is especially enlightening in this connection.

To Paint the Portrait of a Bird*

First paint a cage
with an open door
paint next
something pretty
something simple
something beautiful
something useful
for the bird
next place the canvas against a tree
in a garden
in a park
or in a forest
hide behind the tree
without saying anything
without moving . . .
Sometimes the bird comes quickly
but he can as well take a long time
to make up his mind
Do not be discouraged
wait
wait if necessary for years
the speed or slowness of the bird's coming
not having any relation
to the success of the painting
When the bird comes
if he comes
observe the most profound silence
wait until the bird enters the cage
and when he has entered
close the door softly with the brush
then
erase one by one all the bars
being careful not to touch the bird's feathers
Make next the portrait of the tree

* Original French text of this translation appears on page 153.

choosing the most beautiful of its branches
for the bird
paint also the green foliage and the coolness of the wind
the dust of the sun
and the sound of the creatures of the grass in the
    summer heat
and then wait until the bird decides to sing
If the bird doesn't sing
it's a bad sign
a sign that the painting is bad
but if he sings it's a good sign
a sign that you can sign it
Then you pull out very gently
one of the bird's plumes
and you write your name in a corner of the painting.

At first this poem appears to be only a fanciful paradox, but it contains hints toward a kind of negative theory of art which has correspondences with Prévert's attitude toward language. The lonely lover in *Dans ma maison* and the children in *Le Cancre* and *Page d'écriture* juggle words and eventually separate them from the sensations they are supposed to represent. Words and numbers cannot replace reality; neither can paints on a canvas. Therefore, to paint a bird, one must use a real bird. And for the real bird to sing, one must paint a background so real that the sound of the wind can be heard. To attempt to adhere strictly to such a standard of ultra-realism would mean inevitable failure, but Prévert does not mean all art is doomed.

Both Fay and Noel Arnaud consider this poem Prévert's *ars poetica*, but neither defines precisely what principles it contains. Arnaud says merely that the painter's efforts end in nothing, for the bird flies away, forever unattainable.

It is obvious that, the painting completed, the bird is no longer there. Since he sang, he is free, he freed himself. And since the painting was the cage (destroyed) and the bird (flown), there is no more painting, there is no longer anything.[33]

Yet the poem itself is, like a painting, an attempt to make an image of something. If one cannot paint birds, how can one write poems about the attempt to do so? One can, perhaps, by refusing to be serious: The way to paint a bird in the tradition of pure, denotative Realism, Prévert suggests slyly, is to catch a real bird. This suggestion, in its absurdity, escapes that very tradition of Realism and is therefore something truly created. It is a flight of the imagination, not reality.

This is a theory much like the surrealist one, in which the personal imagination and the unconscious distort or reorder reality according to individual will or whim. The painters Prévert mentions in his poems and seems to admire: Picasso, Miró, and Klee, can all be related to Surrealism. Prévert himself, it has been noted, once was affiliated with Breton's group. It is true that Prévert does not restrict himself to the nonrepresentational treatment of subjects. Many of his poems are in direct contradiction to such a code, e.g., *La Grasse Matinée, Déjeuner du matin, Ravages de la délicatesse* (*Spectacle*, 139). Often, however, Prévert turns to literary collages (*Inventaire*) and subjective splattering and smearing with words, or he openly mocks the language that is supposedly a medium through which to portray the "real."

Two poems written about Picasso and his work may help one to define an esthetic position for the poet. In *Promenade de Picasso* (*Paroles*, 279), Prévert again seems to deny art as a mirror of reality. A painter of "reality" tries vainly to render an apple, but the fruit "disguises itself as a lovely, disguised fruit" and calls forth so many associations, historical and literary, that the painter despairs and falls asleep. Then Picasso, who evidently is not a painter of "reality," passes by and, seeing the apple, eats it. The apple says "Thank you," and Picasso smashes the plate and goes away, leaving the painter only the "terrifying seeds of reality."

Again, a derisory, unserious poem brings up an urgent question: If one cannot paint birds or apples realistically, how *does* one paint them? Perhaps the poem *Lanterne magique de Picasso* supplies an answer to the question, for it deals directly with the painter's work. In *Promenade* nothing is said of Picasso's own work; he only takes a walk and eats an apple, destroying the subject matter of painters of "reality." *Lanterne*, however, tries to translate Picasso into a poetic equivalent. It uses the inventory technique, paralleling Picasso's grouping of subjects in which the stuff of the world is tossed only apparently helter-skelter on the canvas. It uses radical metaphor to correspond to grotesque distortion in drawing. There are the blatant personifications of childhood, as there are houses with eyes or machines with mouths in many surrealist paintings.

PICASSO'S MAGIC LANTERN*

All of a woman's eyes in play in the same picture
The features of the beloved one hunted down by fate under the immobile flower of a sordid painted paper
The white grass of murder in a forest of chairs
A beggar of a torn-open carton on a marble counter
Cigar ashes on the station platform
The portrait of a portrait
The mystery of a child
The undeniable splendor of a table of food
The sudden beauty of a rag in the wind
The insane terror of the trap in a bird's look
The absurd whinnies of a gored horse
The impossible music of bellwether mules
The bull put to death crowned with hats
The redhead asleep whose legs are never a pair and the very large ear of her most minor cares
Perpetual motion caught in the hand
The immense stone statue of a grain of sea salt
The joy of everyday and the uncertainty of dying and the steel of love's way in the wound of a smile
The furthest removed star of the most humble of dogs
And salted in a shop window the tender taste of bread
The good-luck line lost and found again and broken and patched up again decorated with the blue rags of necessity
The dizzy apparition of a Malaga grape on a rice cake
A man in a shack knocking down his homesickness with shots of red wine
And the blinding glow of a cluster of candles
By the sea a window open like an oyster
A horseshoe the naked foot of an umbrella
The incomparable grace of a turtle dove all alone in a very chilly house

* Original French text of this translation appears on page 154.

The dead weight of a pendulum and its lost moments
The sun in somnambulism which wakes with a start in the midst of
   the night Sleeping Beauty suddenly full-blown who throws over
   her shoulder the mantelpiece and draws it along into the masked
   black smoke of Spanish white draped in paper stick-ons
And so many things more
A guitar of green wood rocking the infancy of art
A railway ticket with all its baggage
The hand which clears away a face which faces down a clearing
The snuggling squirrel of a girl new and nude
Splendid smiling happy and immodest
Surging all of a sudden from a bottle cabinet or a music stand like a
   panoply of plants bright green and phallic
It also emerging all of a sudden from the rotting trunk of
A nostalgic academic palm tree desperately old beautiful as an
   antique
And the glass plant covers of morning broken by the cry of an evening
   paper
The terrifying claws of a crab emerging from under a basket
The last blossom of a tree with the two last drops of water for the
   condemned man
And the too-beautiful bride alone and forsaken on the red divan of
   jealousy by the pale fear of her first husbands
And then in a winter garden on the back of a throne an alarmed cat
   and the moustache of her tail under the nostrils of a king
The quicklime of a look in the stone face of an old woman seated
   near a wicker basket
And clutching the wet red lead of the guard rail of an all-white
   lighthouse the two hands blue with cold of a wandering clown who
   looks at the sea and the sea's white horses sleeping in the setting
   sun then waking up with muzzles foaming eyes phosphorescent
   maddened by the glimmer of the lighthouse and its terrifying re-
   volving light
And in a beggar's mouth the well-roasted lark
A crazy young nurse in a public garden who smiling a twisted mechanical smile rocking in her arms a lethargic child traces in the
   dust with her dirty naked foot the silhouette of the father and his
   lost profiles and shows her ragged newborn to passersby Now see
   my handsome one see my lovely one my dream of dreams my
   natural son in one way it's a boy and in another way it's a girl every
   morning he cries but every night I comfort her and I wind them
   both up like a clock
And also fascinated by the twilight the watchman of the block

The life of a spider suspended by a thread

The insomnia of a doll with broken counterweight and her big glass eyes wide-open forever

The death of a white horse the youth of a sparrow

The door of a schoolhouse on Lodi Bridge Street

And the Great Augustines impaled on the iron fence of a house on a little street whose name they bear

All the fishermen of Antibes around a single fish

The violence of an egg the distress of a soldier

The oppressive troublesome presence of a key hidden under a doormat

And the line of sight and the line of death in the plump authoritative hand of a shadow of a man obese and delirious sticking out his tongue carefully behind exemplary designs and the scaled draped crucifixes perpetually erected spectacularly on the large mortuary balcony of the museum of horrors and honors of war the ridiculous living statue of his little short legs and his long bust but not managing despite his sweet smile of a grandiose magnanimous Caudillo to hide the irremediable and pitiable signs of fear of boredom of hate and bastardliness engraved on his mask of pale tawny meat like the obscene graffiti of megalomania engraved by the lamentable torturers of the new order in the urinals of night

And behind him in the charnel house of a half-open diplomatic brief case the mere corpse of a poor peasant attacked in his fields by impeccable money men with a gold bullion barrage

And close by on a table an open grenade with a whole town inside

And all the suffering of that town leveled and bled white

And the home guard prancing all around a stretcher

Where a dead gypsy still dreams

And all the rage of an amorous, working, carefree and charming people which all at once bursts out abruptly like the red cry of a rooster whose throat is slit in public

And the solar specter of low-salaried men which surges up all bloody from the bloody entrails of a worker's house holding at arm's length the poor glimmer of misery the bloody lantern of Guernica and discloses in the broad daylight of its harsh true light the frightful false shades of a faded world worn threadbare stripped to the bone

Of a world dead on its feet

Of a world condemned

And already forgotten

Drowned charred in the thousand fires of the running water of the popular stream

Where the popular blood runs tirelessly

[74]

A Poetry of Anti-Poetry

Inexhaustibly
In the arteries and in the veins of earth and in the arteries and in the
  veins of its true children
And the face of any one of its children simply sketched on a sheet of
  white paper
The face of André Breton the face of Paul Éluard
The face of a wagon driver glimpsed in the street
The flash of a wink from a flower marketer
The blooming smile of a chestnut sculptor
And sculpted in plaster a curly plaster sheep really bleating in the
  hand of a plaster shepherd standing up beside a clothes iron
Beside an empty cigar box
Beside a forgotten crayon
Beside Ovid's Metamorphoses
Beside a shoelace
Beside an armchair with legs cut down by the fatigue of years
Beside a door handle
Beside a still life where the infantile dreams of a housewife die in
  agony on the cold stone of a kitchen sink like fish suffocating and
  croaking on burning pebble beaches
And the house shaken from top to bottom by the poor dead fish cries
  of the despairing housewife who is suddenly shipwrecked swept up
  by the tidal waves from the floor goes regrettably to fall on the
  banks of the Seine in the Vert-Galant gardens
And there she sits on a bench idle
And she takes stock
And she doesn't see herself white rotted by memories and scythed
  like wheat
She has one room left a bedroom
And as she is going to play it heads or tails with the vain hope of
  gaining a little time
A great storm bursts in the three-faced glass
With all the flames of the love of life
With all the lightning flashes of animal heat
All the glints of good spirits
And giving the coup de grâce to the house all turned
Burns the bedroom curtains down
And rolling the covers at the foot of the bed in a ball of fire
Discovers smiling before the world entire
The puzzle of love with all its pieces
All its selected pieces selected by Picasso
A lover his mistress one's legs on the other's throat
And their eyes on their hips their hands somewhat all about

Their legs lifted to the sky and their breasts this way that way
The two bodies entwined exchanged caressed
Love beheaded liberated delighted
The abandoned head rolling on the carpet
Ideas forsaken forgotten astray
Put beyond any possibility of doing harm by joy and pleasure
Choleric ideas confounded by colorful love
Earth-covered ideas earth-bound like the poor rats of death sensing
     the coming of the rip-roaring shipwreck of love
Ideas put back in their place at the bedroom door beside the bread
     beside the shoes
Ideas calcified juggled volatilized deidealized
Ideas petrified before the marvelous indifference of an impassioned
     world
Of a world found again
Of a world indisputable and unexplained
Of a world without *savoir-vivre* but full of *joie de vivre*
Of a world sober and drunk
Of a world sad and gay
Tender and cruel
Real and surreal
Terrifying and hilarious
Nocturnal and diurnal
Expected and unexpected
Beautiful as anything you ever saw.

Thus, in keeping with Picasso's own style, around the obscene
sketch of Franco one finds no political polemic but a corona
of stark images which make up a visual allegory.

. . . in the charnel house of a half-open diplomatic brief case the mere
corpse of a poor peasant attacked in his fields by impeccable money
men with a gold bullion barrage

Bankers did not "really" kill a peasant with gold ingots, and the
peasant's corpse could hardly have found its way into a diplomatic briefcase, but in the artist's experience these imaginary
events may symbolize a truth which can only be represented
clearly and forcefully by means of such primitive allegory.

There is more than just haphazard inventory in *Lanterne*.
There are the prévertian social and political attitudes; sadistic

militarism, for example, is again associated with capitalist oppression, as in the lines quoted above. The harsh facts of the misery of Guernica cannot express these attitudes, all highly emotional and all the product of experience, unless such facts are incorporated into symbols created and arranged by the artist. He arranges them according to the nature of his personal vision, not according to the space-time coordinates of "real" events.

Experience, then, of a personal nature, processed by the imagination, is the painter's "subject." A series of mingled impressions and associations, the "stream of imagination," is the true reality of the poet. Impressions of the senses can be confused, distorted, absurd, yet very significant when edited by the free imagination; but they are not *planned* and *executed* as are the impressions of a painter who puts an apple on a plate and sets out deliberately to match its color, form, and texture. This deliberate imitation is a distortion of one kind of reality, the reality of the interaction of environment and imagination.

The imagination itself operates on a dynamo of emotion. Many lines of *Lanterne* show Prévert's sympathy with the Spanish painter's belief in the superior energy of that dynamo. Picasso paints "the mystery of a child" and "the sudden beauty of a rag in the wind" rather than a child or a rag divested of all one's emotional response to them. He also paints "all the misery of this city" and "all the rage of an amorous working people." But especially it is love, "beheaded, liberated, delighted" that he paints, arranging the eyes, hands, breasts, and legs of the lovers as he sees fit, for it is the nature of the emotion, not its vessels, he strives to capture.

Judging by the number and kind of formal statements Picasso has made about his art, the painter also believes words are often ineffectual as a means of representing feelings. His few comments are as paradoxical as Prévert's, and they reveal a striking number of parallels with the poet's creed as it has been roughly outlined here. Both painter and poet emphasize emotional rather than intellectual responses. Both believe in spontaneous, changing creation rather than calculated craftsmanship. And both deny the artist any apocalyptic role.

One remembers the bird in its anti-intellectual stance when reading this paragraph of Picasso's:

Everyone wants to understand art. Why not try to understand the song of a bird? Why does one love the night, flowers, everything around one, without trying to understand them? But in the case of painting, people have to *understand*. If only they would realize above all that an artist works of necessity, that he himself is only a trifling bit of the world, and that no more importance should be attached to him than to plenty of other things which please us in the world, though we can't explain them.[34]

And Picasso would probably agree with Prévert's sleight of hand in the painting of the bird, the erasing of the cage, and the flight of the bird, which signify the transcendence of the real.

There is no abstract art. You must always start with something. Afterward you can remove all traces of reality. There's no danger then, anyway, because the idea of the object will have left an indelible mark. It is what started the artist off, excited his ideas, and stirred up his emotions. Ideas and emotions will in the end be prisoners in his work. Whatever they do, they can't escape from the picture.[35]

They speak of naturalism in opposition to modern painting. I would like to know if anyone has ever seen a natural work of art. Nature and art, being two different things, cannot be the same thing. Through art we express our conception of what nature is not.[36]

Though they do not make up a dogma, for there are too many paradoxes and too many flippancies in them, the Prévert poems on art, and particularly on Picasso, yield a few very general and very flexible principles of esthetics. A concentration of the emotions of the individual, the free play of the imagination energized by those emotions, and a rejection of any "reality" which does not bear the mark of the artist's personality are the most basic of these principles. In the next chapter, the relation of this loose credo to Prévert's inimitable styles becomes of primary importance.

CHAPTER 4

Styles: A Poetry of Plain Talk

In a very general way the titles of Prévert's books of poetry help define his styles: *Paroles* because the poet has a genius for making all sorts of ordinary idiom highly expressive, *Spectacle* because his verbal tricks often correspond to the antics of a clown or a magician, and *La Pluie et le beau temps* because the emotional tones of his symbols can have the classic simplicity of the summer-and-winter, sunshine-and-rain cycle of life and love. In more direct terms, this language is sometimes common and colloquial, even vulgar (but rarely banal), sometimes zany in its arrangement of images or in its boldness of metaphor, and occasionally lyric, in the tradition of the *cri du coeur*.

Already we are faced with variety that amounts almost to contradiction. That is the reason for discussing *styles* of Prévert rather than *the* style. Though his work is usually uniquely his own, the poet also represents a synthesis of several currents in modern poetry. Some of his work, written in the language of the streets, captures the instinctive rhythms of Parisian dialect, the music inherent in the tongue, and at the same time strips away any hint of "poetic" diction or rhetoric. Thus he belongs both to a line of very ancient poets, the medieval *jongleurs* who sang poems and did not write them—and a good share of Prévert's poems have been set to music—and to a group of twentieth-century poets, like Bertolt Brecht, George Brassens, and Raymond Queneau, who are striving to recover the lilt of street songs and speech. This *colloquialism* is the most salient stylistic quality of Prévert.

But in other poems the reader will not only miss the syntax of common speech, he will discover no syntax whatever. There are several rather long Prévert poems which are only "inventories" (the most famous of these poems bears that name), in which images, without verbs or connecting conjunctions, are strung in a pattern which can either suggest meaning or be amusingly absurd. The Prévert inventory is made up of *things*, apparently evoked arbitrarily; stones, the sun, pins, elephants, armchairs—and several raccoons. It is the intuitive ordering of images to achieve an emotional effect, rather than the reasoned organization of "thought" with an esthetic frosting.

The inventory technique, along with certain others, appears to derive from the poet's experience with the Surrealist movement. *Contre-pied*, a sort of elaborate slip of the tongue ("A rope hunter with a head dancer"), the pun, *double-entendre*, and nonsense rhymes are all techniques depending on psychological phenomena which Surrealists incorporated into a poetic method. Claiming the unconscious as the source of the truly poetic image,[1] that is, the image undistorted by the censorship of rational processes, the Surrealists tried to liberate such images through "automatic writing."[2] Switched modifiers, inadvertent puns, and nonsense syllables may be confusing "mistakes" in the *rational* thinking process, but the Surrealists cultivated them as legitimate poetic devices, because of, rather than in spite of, their irrational or absurd quality.

Prévert's use of these methods betrays a creative process much more sophisticated than automatic writing; he is certainly no babbler. But, even employed deliberately rather than accidentally, such devices retain a spontaneous, nonrational character. Indeed, to use them effectively, a poet must cede some of his rational control over words.[3] Left by themselves to form odd cross-breeds somewhere in the darkness of the unconscious, words can emerge in original patterns with an inherent poetic energy. Such images—spontaneous, not integrated logically into the poem, often pure whim—mark another characteristic Prévert style.

Occasionally, although he does not become effusively decorative, Prévert writes a love poem or a song using conventional imagery in more or less regular verse patterns, including the traditional Alexandrine. In *Pour toi mon amour*, for example, the lover approaches his beloved with flowers, pet birds, and, finally, chains; in *Le Miroir brisé* (*Paroles*, 205) the principal image is the old one of the lanced and bleeding heart of a stricken swain. The rhyme scheme in these poems is irregular, but certain stanzas, like old *rondeaux* or children's rhymes, repeat the same syllable at the end of several consecutive short lines, a technique which, in keeping with Prévert's attitude toward his art, is one of the most naïve and "natural" of poetic devices.

Oranges and the sun, metaphors for woman in Prévert's pro-love poems, have unity, simple form and color. These are also the qualities one finds in a number of very brief, highly elliptical poems which treat the love theme. The phrases in these poems, as naked as verbal images can be, without sentence framework of subject and verb, may well remind one of another influence on modern poetry; namely, that of imagist doctrines and the *haiku* verse forms from the Japanese tradition. Certainly, two broad aspects of such poetry, economy of expression and concreteness of imagery, can define many of Prévert's poems, especially those of a page or less in length. Thus one may distinguish in Prévert a third and a fourth stylistic mode: one introduces chiefly stark, concrete images, often swiftly extended into metaphor; the other offers figures of popular currency couched in simple, lyrical verse forms.

A final and pervasive quality in Prévert's work, one that appears to have some effect on all of his other styles, may result from his knowledge of the techniques of the modern cinema. Almost every critic who studies Prévert closely eventually uses the camera as a metaphor for the poet's style. The metaphor applies because the movie camera is both an instrument of objective documentation and a "magic lantern" able to trick the eye and imagination. Although Prévert can and does play with sounds and words, his work generally impresses one as being highly visual and dramatic. Of course, in many poems the music and the image are as inseparable as a film and its sound track. But the eye is more taken than the ear. Perhaps this is the nature of the film art too; the name "talkie" soon disappeared, but the colloquialism "picture" remains.

When critics speak of "anti-poetry" they seem to mean a poetry which scorns a hieratic or apocalyptic role as well as the frozen forms and artificial, literary language of traditional verse.

The late Symbolists, beginning at Mallarmé's apogee of esoterism, assumed the position of occult priests, and their language became subtle, indirect, and finally hermetic.[4] In the twentieth century, the Dadaist and Surrealist writers revolted against the heritage of the Romantics and Symbolists, and even against "art" itself.[5] Then, once the anarchic fervor of Dada had dissipated itself into chaos or silence and the Surrealists had found a priest of their own in Breton and had begun to evolve a complex dogma, a few poets kept on developing new modes of expression without pretentions to oracular authority.

One of these modes was a simple, direct, yet imaginative poetry which drew much from the vocabulary and rhythm of the spoken language. Guillaume Apollinaire, father of so many diverse schools of poetry, and Max Jacob fostered this prosaic style,[6] although at the turn of the century Francis Jammes, Verhaeren and the Naturists had already renounced orthodox Symbolism in favor of more colloquial diction and homelier themes.[7] Writers after 1915, perhaps partly influenced by the revolutionary spirit of Surrealism, have often turned away from "pure" poetry, a mathematics of the soul, to concentrate on the tangible and its expression in a language people really use.

According to Picon, this "poetry of non-poetry" represents "the last great poetic event" in contemporary literature.[8] He defines such poetry as the inverse of the art-for-art's sake theory which lurks behind many post-Symbolist doctrines, postulating that this new poetry is more concerned with raw life than with itself.

Formerly, the poet made his poetry with what others abandoned as non-poetic; he poeticized the universe. Today he makes poetry with what he knows to be non-poetic: he de-poeticizes the poem. It is no longer a matter of annexing what is real to poetry, but of annexing poetry to what is real.[9]

On more than one count Prévert qualifies as a major figure in this current of nonpoetry. His concentration on contemporary social and political topics is a marked departure from the self-conscious art of the Symbolists. Also, he mocks the diction and theory of "pure" poetry much as the Surrealists did, but he often chooses, as an alternative, everyday turns of speech rather than the odd, rambling, and disconnected style of "automatic writing."

But as a number of critics have implied, the *poésie parlée* of Prévert has a purity of its own. It satirizes journalese and commercial jargon, the cheapest, most corrupt popular language, and prunes away all but a cryptic, colorful core of street talk. For this reason, the poet has been called a hygienist of language—one who cleans away all but the simple, common, and uniquely apt expression.[10]

The dramatic character of much of the poet's work gives him occasion to introduce quoted speech, and Prévert has great talent in mimicking dialogue. Even poems without direct exchanges between speaking characters are written almost as dramatic monologues. The poem *Barbara*, for example, despite random rhyme and the use of the refrain ("Remember, Barbara"), sounds like someone reminiscing aloud. This personal point of view permits the shock line "What a screwed-up war," for it passes as a *cri du coeur*, the nonliterary man's shout of rage against the holocaust of war. Similarly, in *Dîner de têtes*, which of course contains many speeches and asides, some of the "descriptive" passages are deliberate parodies of certain speech mannerisms: "It was really exquisitely charming and in such good taste that when the President arrived with a sumptuous Columbus egg head it was positively ecstatic." This vocabulary and this gross but ineffective adverbial exaggeration appear in the everyday language, as readers of society pages in daily newspapers know.

Profanity, slang, and rude puns also mark the poetry as colloquial. In the poem *Le Temps des noyaux* (*Paroles*, 84) the oldsters on the Metro of life ask if the young will "descend" at the next stop—which is war in the metaphorical voyage. Youth replies in the negative and decides instead to "descend" the remnants of the preceding generation. The verb *descendre*, when used transitively and colloquially, means to "drop" with a bullet or blow. To any protests from the old, the young reply, "Bouclez-la vieillards!" In comparable English slang, the message is "Button your lips, old-timers."

But the relation of Prévert's poetic talk to real speech goes beyond mere similarities in diction; the rhythm and pattern of lines correspond in many instances to the cadence of conversation.

The number of lines which begin with "and," when that conjunction is certainly not needed for clarity or grammatical correctness, indicates the poet's attention to the details of spoken sentence structure. In the poem *Dans ma maison* the phrase "Et puis . . ." helps to characterize the naïve, childlike lover, who always uses the simplest conjunctions in profusion, linking ideas indiscriminately. Similarly, there are eighteen lines in the short poem *Page d'écriture*, also about children, which begin with "and," so that the narration itself has the rapid, breathless pace of a child's chatter.

Poems like *Familiale* reveal Prévert's skill in putting talk into poetic form. The emphatic repetitions, expletives, and ellipses make the whole tone of the poem colloquial, yet the hammering rhyme and refrain are not to be found in ordinary speech, unless one counts accidental "poet-and-don't-know-it" discoveries.

> Et le père qu'est-ce qu'il fait le père?
> Il fait des affaires
> Sa femme fait du tricot
> Son fils la guerre
> Lui des affaires

The first line of this citation could be written, with equivalent "meaning," "Que fait le père?" but the colloquial lilt of the phrase, and a certain dramatic flavor as well, would be lost. The next two lines, absolutely bare, flat statements, contrast well as responses to the question with a flair. In the fourth line the verb is deleted, and in the last the verb is absent and the subject is in the colloquial, disjunctive form, so that the ironic contrast between gravity of meaning and nonchalance in delivery becomes even sharper; the family activities are discussed in what is much like a conversation between strangers on a train. Yet the rhyme remains and occurs with increasing frequency until the climactic end of the poem. Perhaps the extremely laconic structure of the poem in some way justifies the overrich rhymes; at any rate, *Familiale* succeeds in being both speech and poetry without seeming self-contradictory.

The colloquial style of Prévert can be dominant or subordinate in any one poem to another of his styles, but it is one of the most constant strains in his work. That he has written children's books and popular songs perhaps indicates a predilection for simple, musical language, but even if *Paroles* were the only evidence, one would have to describe Prévert's anti-poetry principally as a return to the commonplace as subject matter and to common speech as its vehicle.

CHAPTER 5

Surrealist Remnants

Certain other qualities in Prévert belong in part to the tradition of Surrealism. A spirit of revolt and an infatuation with wordplay link his work with Surrealist theory and practice.[11] In addition, the irrationality of Prévert, his scorn for anything intellectual, signals a certain kinship with the Surrealist's hostility toward the conscious mind as a poetic instrument. And, finally, certain minor traits of style in individual poems indicate that Prévert has some technical mannerisms in common with his early associates.

To discuss the traces of Surrealist method in Prévert one must recognize the peculiar temper of the revolt that inspired Surrealism and its immediate predecessors, Dada, Cubism, and Futurism. The Surrealist revolt, like the Dada revolt, was primarily a revolt against traditional forms of rational discourse, including traditional literature.[12] It was a form of anti-poetry in which grotesque humor supplanted sentiment expressed in conventional poetic formulas.[13] Humor and revolt are similarly combined in Prévert, who mocks more polite poetry by means of excessive rhyme, alliteration, and wordplay, and who deliberately chooses images which are amusing in proportion to their absurdity.

Apollinaire and Max Jacob also belong at the source of this Surrealist style. It was Apollinaire who coined the term "surrealism" in 1917, and the later Surrealists have claimed him as a forerunner in their literary revolt.[14] He and Jacob, while reaffirming the poetic worth of prosaic simplicity and economy, also introduced novel punctuation, wordplay, and elliptical syntax.[15] Jacob was particularly adept at punning and alliteration. At times he seems almost slapstick. Consider this title of one of his short pieces: *Fausses Nouvelles! Fosses Nouvelles!*[16] (Literally "False Reports! New Graves!" A not dissimilar English version might be "Grave News! New Graves!") or this excerpt from *Avenue du Maine*, an effective translation of which is impossible:

> Les manèges déménagent
> Ménager manager
> De l'avenue du Maine
> Qui ton manège mène
> Pour mener ton ménage!
> Ménage ton ménage
> Manège ton manège
> Ménage ton manège
> Manège ton ménage.[17]

Compare this buffoonery with Prévert's tiny jest of a poem, *L'Amiral*, which contains both a pun and extravagant alliteration.

THE ADMIRAL

> Admiral Arimewith
> Arimewith what
> A rime with nothing
> Admiral Arimewith
> Admiral nothing.

> L'amiral Larima
> Larima quoi
> La rime à rien
> L'amiral Larima
> L'amiral Rien.[18]

Humor in the twentieth-century poetic revolt, heralded by Apollinaire and Jacob, is mostly of a mocking, derisive kind.[19] Prévert, too, usually twists language with a deliberate intent to ridicule or insult; even in his poems apparently composed of harmless verbal pranks there is an implied mockery of conventional poetry. Now and then a reader finds passages which are certainly mere tomfoolery with words, in the style of Dada, but Prévert can give an impression of *désinvolture* while keeping a keen edge of satire.

One of the best known examples of a humorous, surrealist technique in Prévert is the poem *Inventaire*. Léon Gros sees this work, which is composed simply of a list of things, as an attempt to ridicule traditional poetry and at the same time as a "denunciation of the absurdity of the world."[20] That the odd juxtaposition of images and the utter disregard for the connectives of logical discourse imply an impudent comment on conventional verse goes without saying, but one might argue that far from denouncing the absurdity of the world the poem celebrates it. Surrealist poets, believing in the primacy of the unconscious and the truth of the disordered, apparently irrelevant images which arise from it, would probably interpret the poem as one of their indirect offspring, a work composed of a stream of words having only subtle, subterranean relationships. The poem indeed has a certain helter-skelter appearance, which tempts one to consider it as "automatic writing." But many of the combinations of images seem too meaningful to be unpremeditated.

INVENTORY*

One stone
two houses
three ruins
four gravediggers
a garden
some flower blooms

one raccoon

one dozen oysters one lemon one loaf bread
one ray of sunshine
one ground swell
six musicians
one door with doormat
one gentleman with a legion of honor festoon

another raccoon

one sculptor who sculpts Napoleons
the flower called marigold
two lovers on a big bed

* Original French text of this translation appears on page 159.

one tax collector one chair three turkeys
one priest one boil
one wasp
one floating kidney
one racing stable
one unworthy heir two dominican brothers three grasshoppers one
  folding chair
two girls of easy virtue one uncle from Cyprus
One Mother of Sorrows three sugar daddies two of M. Seguin's goats
one Louis XV heel
one Louis XVI armchair
one Henry II buffet, two Henry III buffets, three buffets Henry IV
one lopsided drawer
one ball of string two safety pins one old gentleman
one winged Victory of Samothrace one accountant two assistant ac-
  countants a man of the world two surgeons three vegetarians
one cannibal
one colonial expedition one whole horse one half-pint of good blood
  one tsetse fly
one lobster American style one French garden
two English apples
one lorgnette one footman one orphan one iron lung
one day of glory
one week of goodness
one month of Mary
one terrible year
one minute of silence
one second of negligence
and . . .

five or six raccoons

one little boy who goes into the schoolhouse crying
one little boy who comes out of the schoolhouse laughing
one ant
two flintstones
seventeen elephants one probate judge on vacation sitting on a deck
  chair
one countryside with a lot of green grass in it
one cow
one bull
two fine loves three large organs one Marengo veal
one Austerlitz sun
one seltzer-water siphon

one glass of white wine lemon twist
one Tom Thumb one last pardon one stone Calvary one rope ladder
two latin sisters three dimensions twelve apostles a thousand and one
   nights thirty-two positions six sections of the world five cardinal
   points ten years of good and loyal service seven capital sins two
   fingers of the hand ten drops before every meal thirty days in
   prison of which fifteen are in solitary five minute intermission
and . . .

several raccoons.

Although in writing of the devices of inventory and *contrepied*,
Bataille speaks of "associations" and of their leveling, anti-poetic
function,[21] he insists that they stem from Surrealist methods and
remain "a form of automatism."[22] Queval equivocally states that
the inventory trick is the style of Prévert which "most nearly
approaches automatism."[23] Nadeau merely suggests that through
close analysis the critic may discover "laws more mysterious than
those of logic or mere utility."[24] But, though it seems a vast
junkyard, museum and zoo all haphazardly combined, this poem
illustrates Prévert's method of grouping items in a far from
random disorder. There is often a planned and highly expressive
"absurdity" in his arrangement—or disarrangement—of words,
and this planned confusion distinguishes Prévert's inventory
from the experiments of Breton and Soupalt, who refused to
edit the flow of images from the subconscious.

There is compressed history, for example, in the progression
of the first six lines of *Inventaire*. From raw matter (stone), man
makes houses which he reduces to ruins; then he dies and returns
to dust (via the gravediggers), and the garden runs to flowers
over his grave. Perhaps something of Prévert's whole view of the
world lies behind this progression. After the ludicrous construc-
tions of man there will still be flowers and raccoons, which, being free and natural, the poet admires.

Depending on the reader to make his own associations, the inventory technique operates as a weapon of subtle satire. To
express his contempt for the Church, and to make fun of its high
seriousness, Prévert merely juxtaposes a reference to the sacred
and another reference to the scatological or to the pornographic:

> two latin Sisters three dimensions
> twelve apostles a thousand and one nights
> thirty-two positions . . .

This sort of innuendo, sly rather than fortuitous, indicates more control of the mind than the tenets of Dada or Surrealism would admit. Marcel Raymond, in his study of Surrealism and its precursors, says that Dadaist work "gives the reader a more striking impression of incoherence,"[25] and that most Surrealist texts "disclose an incessant flow of images whose common characteristic is that they defy common sense."[26] Though not entirely free of such images, Prévert's work usually possesses a degree of malice or of approval which gives it direction without sacrificing the fresh, spontaneous gait of Surrealist style.

The inventory technique, the pun, and *contre-pied* are among "the great structures, the great arteries, the constants of this language," according to Queval.[27] *Contre-pied*, in which the familiar modifiers in two clichés are switched, also stems from Surrealist experiments, being a kind of highly complicated slip of the tongue.[28] But, as in the case of the inventory technique, Prévert elaborates beyond the point of automatism. "Sought fortuity," neither logical nor unconscious, may perhaps describe his method.

Cortège (*Paroles*, 273), one of the poet's most popular poems, illustrates admirably the use of *contre-pied* as a means of ridiculing the same old Prévert puppets. Though the verbal "finds" in this poem recall Surrealist experiments, they fall into a very deliberate disorder, one "calculated to produce maximum violence."[29] To be sure, there is no mistaking the barb in almost every phrase: some are directed against the Church (A little Bengal sister with a Tiger of Saint Vincent de Paul); others against intellectuals (A member of the prostate with a hypertrophy of the French Academy). Written in a Surrealist style it may be, but *Cortège* is not a pure Surrealist poem; it appears to be cleverly calculated to achieve certain effects, and in it *contre-pied* becomes a tool of stinging satire, not a result of psychological experiment.[30]

The American critic Eliot Fay understates the matter considerably when he says that Prévert "does not hesitate to introduce

unusual words or to invent new words, and he relishes an occa-
sional pun."[31] The poet does not hesitate, certainly, to introduce
unusual words; he rather goes out of his way to wrench terms
out of familiar contexts and to put them into new ones. And it
would be more appropriate to say that Prévert cannot *refrain*
from punning. There are Prévert poems made up of so many
unusual words or puns that a translator must give them up or
spoil them with a footnote.

Sometimes the pun may have a definite relationship to the
structure of the poem, as in *La Grasse Matinée*, when the phrase
"café-crème" suggests to the starving man "café-crime," an association which foreshadows the murder for bread. And occasionally a pun can be the whole point of the poem, as in *L'Accent
grave* (*Paroles*, 68) or *Le Discours sur la paix* (*Paroles*, 259).
This latter poem illustrates one of the poet's favorite tricks:
dredging up a submerged metaphor and interpreting it literally.
Thus the politician "stumbles" upon a "hollow phrase," falls into
it, and is unable to extricate himself before the auditors guess
his true intent.

At other times, however, Prévert seems merely to decorate his
main theme with clever but irrelevant wordplay. Particularly
in his longer poems, which are almost always fantasy reminis-
cent of Surrealist drama as it descends from *Ubu Roi*, Prévert
interrupts the narrative with passages of explosive verbal mis-
chief. The words seem to run away from the world of dictionary
referents and perform stunts for their own amusement. So, in
Dans ma maison, the childlike lover realizes abruptly that the
words man attaches to things are arbitrarily chosen, and only
convention prohibits one from saying "A band of bonapartes
passes by in the desert/The emperor is called Dromedary."

Other types of wordplay appear in these passages of verbal
fireworks; in fact the poet employs almost every imaginable form
of buffoonery with language, even the tongue-twister. "Pope
Pius' papa's pipe is putrid." ("La pipe au papa du Pape Pie
pue."[32]) "Playing with words is by the way one of Prévert's greatest joys . . ." is Gaudin's fair assessment of the importance of
this aspect of the poet.[33] The critic adds that alliteration and
assonance are the sources of the greatest variety of effects. He
might also have added rhyme, which Prévert uses not only for

emphasis and lyric effect but also as a humorous device. An example is the snowballing rhyme in the middle of *Dîner de têtes.*

Calmed down a little, she next lets her look of a lonely woman wander over the table and seeing among the hors-d'oeuvres some smoked herring, she takes some, not caring, with tearful bearing, then gets the rest, thinking of the admiral who, as a living guest, wasn't so obsessed with their zest and nevertheless thought them the best. Stop.

Thus, through a great many poems run glints and sometimes broad streaks of the sort of humor, often based on wordplay and often covertly rebellious, that characterizes Surrealism. The second of Prévert's poetic personae, the Harlequin, alternates with the laconic, straight-talking man from the streets. Sometimes on the same page the newspaper, the telegraph message, the old lullaby, the blooper, the wisecrack, and the court fool's barbed absurdities join in a cacophonous uproar; but the confusion is not meaningless, as were the dizzy tantrums of some earlier, more violent schools of poetry. The range, variety, and daring of Prévert's language, and his ingenuity in scrambling sounds, words, and images result in the birth of a poetry "very new and very original."[34] The praise seems just. Even recognizing a certain debt to Surrealist prototypes, a critic may consider Prévert's clowning with words, at once *cocasserie* (extravaganza) and biting satire, as his most inventive personal style.

CHAPTER 6

Images and Lyrics

We have noted two principal styles in Prévert's work: The simple, colloquial phrases of the "common man," and the highly imaginative linguistic stunts of an uncommon comic. They occur together, as in the speeches of the man's head man in *Dîner de têtes*, but they also diverge rather sharply as poetic approaches to the world. In some of Prévert's love poems, other styles contrast almost as strikingly: these poems may consist of a few, spare phrases; or they may be catchy popular tunes. The poetry of plain talk and that of word-juggling both stem from an atmosphere of poetic revolt; they are either overtly or by implication "anti-poetry." A few of Prévert's love lyrics, on the other hand, do not mock conventional symbols or the traditional forms of versification but make moderate use of them.

Lyric poetry in France has a long and honorable tradition, and the work of Prévert in many ways constitutes a return to the style of some of the very earliest masters of song. Knowing of Prévert's sympathy with criminals, tramps, and mischievous, libertine youth, and recognizing his use of the vocabulary of such characters, one cannot help comparing him with another "underworld" poet, François Villon. Even the manner in which Prévert's early efforts circulated about Paris during the occupation, by handmade copy and by word of mouth, reminds one of the way Villon's fame spread; for the medieval vagabond's verses were sung from tavern to tavern among those who probably could not read.

And if Prévert's lovers are usually poor people in city slums, often roustabouts and streetwalkers, he nevertheless sings to them of flowers, rain, and blue sky—the customary furniture of the poetry of romance from Ronsard to Verlaine. Further, he sings to them in more or less traditional verse forms. *Tournesol* (*Spectacle*, 198), a simple celebration of springtime, a girl, and a flower, contains alternate six-syllable lines which are read very much like the *hémistiches* of regular Alexandrines, and also flexible full Alexandrines in which mute *e*'s are either pronounced or suppressed. The six-syllable lines employ assonance, whereas the Alexandrines always rhyme, though not in a precise pattern.

SUNFLOWER*

Every day of the week
In winter and autumn
In Paris skies by day
The factory chimneys smoke only gray

But springtime arrives, a flower over his ear
On his arm a pretty girl
Sunflower Sunflower
That's the name of the flower
The nickname of the girl
She has no first name, no last name either
Dances on street corners
At Belleville and Seville

Sunflower Sunflower Sunflower
Waltz of the street corners
And the sunny days come in
The sweet life with them

The genii of the Bastille smokes a blue cigarette
In the amorous air
Of the sky of Seville of the sky of Belleville
And even anywhere
Sunflower Sunflower Sunflower
It's the name of the flower
The nickname of the girl.

* Original French text of this translation appears on page 161.

Prévert also writes of the melancholy and pain of love, the inevitable minor key of lyricists like Musset and Verlaine. Like them, he uses the image of the torn and bleeding heart (See *Le Miroir brisé*, in *Paroles*, 205). One also finds the prison-slave-chains metaphor for the lover's troth (*Chanson du géolier*, in *Paroles*, 216; *Pour toi mon amour*), and, like countless poets for many centuries, Prévert compares the transient beauty of a woman with the freshness of a flower, urging that such beauty be savored early, not allowed to wither (*Le Bouquet*, in *Paroles*, 236). In these poems, as in his brighter love lyrics, there is generally a series of rhymes which, if it is not regular, is yet certainly musical. Thus a great many poems from *Paroles* appeared first as popular songs, and even the love poems in freer forms, according to Gaudin, always possess "a quite markedly 'poetic' character."[35]

Gaudin disagrees both with the hostile critics who accuse Prévert of clumsiness and dissonance[36] and with the apologists like Eugenio de Andrade who excuse the poet on the grounds that he is striving to render the idiom of common, prosaic people.[37] On the contrary, says this critic, Prévert offers a most subtle harmony and interplay of sonorities, a most calculated shift of meters. The reader may fail to notice this because

. . . Prévert chooses to give a popular form to his poems: song, romance, lament; and above all he possesses admirably the art, given to very few, of using popular language without mimicking it.[38]

Two others who have examined Prévert's lyricism at some length, Queval and Bataille, suggest that the poet writes songs and *cris du coeur* which have little to do with what is now called poetry. Poetry which is purely "literary," says Bataille, is a sort of "mutilated song."[39] If such purely literary composition is all of poetry, then Prévert is no poet, but if the ballad, the nursery rhyme, and the anonymous work-song are fundamentally poetic, then he most certainly is one. Almost all of Prévert's work, says Queval, was written to be said or sung aloud, and that is the reason for his great variety in rhythm. In addition, the poet can speak spontaneously under the stress of emotion, with little overt concern for the esthetic or intellectual dimensions of his art.

This kind of *cri du coeur*, Queval admits, may not be literature at all, but the label does not matter in the least so long as the reader is moved. Prévert, he notes, never has tried to write "literature" anyway.[40]

These three critics, Gaudin, Queval, and Bataille, stress the importance of the song in Prévert. Recalling that this musical quality is most often associated with the love theme and that the love stories are about ordinary people enjoying or grieving over simple things, one may conclude that Prévert belongs to a tradition, but it is the ancient one of the ballad and folk song, not the more recent "literary" one.

Colloquial lyricism, however, does not characterize all the love poems in the various collections of verse. Just as plain talk is balanced by elaborate wordplay, the popular tunes about love may be contrasted with another, highly stylized treatment of the same theme. This second style reminds one of the imagist poems of Ezra Pound and his group, and of the Japanese *haiku* forms which influenced them.[41] In these Prévert poems, seldom more than a half dozen lines in length, a situation or scene is compressed into a few phrases; the result might be fairly called "an emotional . . . complex in an instant of time" (though not very complex in Prévert's case).

Poems of this type, like *Alicante*, consist of phrases only. Like Pound's famous lines on the Metro station, they are pictures or images and not narrative, so they lack verbs. Also, in keeping with imagist doctrine, the language is concrete, specific, and economical. The relationship between the phrases, between the objects in the scene, goes unexpressed. An orange on the table, a dress on the carpet, a girl in bed; these things make up a scene, not a cogent story, but there is perhaps an esthetic principle behind their juxtaposition without overt explanation. *Alicante* suggests a metaphor; the woman, like the orange, is disrobed to be enjoyed, and the dress falls like a rind to the floor. *Sanguine*, a later poem included in *Spectacle*, elaborates on an identical figure but expresses the comparison. In the shorter poem, the sight, touch, and taste sensations evoked by the orange seem almost superimposed on the image of the woman; the associations are perhaps more immediate and complete, yet subtler, than those any verb could suggest.

[97]

Like microcosmic "inventories," these imagist poems radiate an emotional force as a result of the juxtaposition of objects in a planned sequence. One is again reminded of the work of certain painters to whom the poet has alluded with respect: the canvases and collages of Picasso, Tanguy, Miró, and Klee often employ a few disparate objects which gain significance in a certain arrangement. And almost all of Prévert's poems in this style are like paintings; they employ principally visual images, separated by a space on the page instead of by conjunctions or semicolons.

In this terse, colorful, highly emotional style, Prévert attains a limit of directness in poetic language. He uses words in a visual as well as in a verbal pattern. There is no literary rhetoric; seldom are there even adjectives; the word stands almost as a thing. It is from this limit, at which language has become as concrete and specific as it can, that the anti-poetry of imaginative, mocking wordplay departs. When the relationship between symbols and their referents, even when presented in static purity, finally fades, the poet begins to twist and disjoin language. He questions words, as the childlike lover waiting in the house questions the sense of the old phrase *gai comme un pinson*. He discovers that if words cannot capture the "real" anymore than a painter can paint a live bird on a canvas, they can evoke a sur-real world where quill pens are transformed into peacocks; a world illogical and fanciful, but one full of powerful, meaningful emotions.

CHAPTER 7

The Camera Eye

The paradox returns: Prévert is a realist, recording the sincere banalities of ordinary people; yet he is equally a surrealist, boldly distorting and exploiting language. The poet's attitude toward his art seems to be divided, and the style he adopts depends on whether he wishes to take language seriously, as a medium capable of rendering sensations more or less accurately, or lightly, as a bin of worn-out toys with which one can make up fascinating new games. The two extremes represented in the styles discussed here, documentary Realism and absurd Surrealism, can perhaps be reconciled if we consider a fifth and more pervasive Prévert style, the *cinematic* one.

Though his theme may be a romantic or even a sentimental one, Prévert's treatment of it often remains impersonal. Romantic poets, claims René Bertelé, tell "what happens to them," whereas Prévert merely tells "what happens."[42] The poet's diction does give one an impression of objectivity. He usually avoids speaking directly to the reader, preferring to present an incident or character type without comments.

Most critics relate this objectivity to Prévert's cinema career. Queval amasses comments by writers sympathetic to this interpretation, and in them the camera metaphor for the poet's style occurs again and again, almost always in connection with his stark, often brutal realism in imagery and idiom.[43] Gaudin, too, contrasts the poetry of plain talk and that of naked, verbless imagery—which he suggests are camera techniques—with wordplay.

Nevertheless let us take care not to exaggerate the importance of word-play in Prévert's poetry: a very great number of his poems, on the contrary, display the barest, most unencumbered art imaginable.

Very often the poem is born from a single, pure sensation or a series of sensations, and Prévert, influenced by the cinema perhaps, seems to limit himself to recording the scene before his eyes, eliminating all rhetoric.[44]

To convey through a poem the emotional impact of this "series of sensations," Gaudin postulates, the poet deliberately chooses very easy, almost neutral words. The language of the poem becomes transparent, like a camera lens, so that the actual event is in perfect focus. If properly "shot," the poem-picture contains nothing purely verbal or literary to usurp the reader's attention or to warp the image when projected.[45]

Superobjectivity, however, does not wholly explain the "miracle" by means of which Prévert's little phrases, "so simple, so stripped of artifice, so free of literary lacework,"[46] move a reader. As Picon and Maurice Nadeau observe in their chapters devoted to Prévert, the cameraman edits and orders images. The cameraman *selects*. If he is successful, gestures and details of décor in a certain sequence reveal the emotions of characters and thus stir those of the spectator.[47]

Picon adds that the artistry of such photographic verse is in the progression of scenes, not in the isolated image.

The poetry is in the pacing—in the act of going from one image to the next, from one object to another object; and the poem is often a cinematic *montage*, a series of *cuttings*.[48]

The emphasis here is on the *dynamic* quality of Prévert's poems, where sparse, concrete images occur in rapid sequence, often alternating with laconic speech. Indeed, the most obvious examples of this method do read like movie scripts. The author gives way to the editor, who documents the meaningful words and actions in an incident and lets them suggest their own emotional truth.

A short poem which both Nadeau and Queval treat as a cinema "take," *Déjeuner du matin*, records slight, external gestures to indicate intense, hidden emotions. The character of these emotions is only suggested, and very subtly at that.[49]

[100]

EARLY BREAKFAST*

He put coffee
In the cup
He put cream
In the cup of coffee
He put sugar
In the coffee cup
With the little spoon
He stirred it up
He tried a sip
He put back the cup
He never spoke
He lit
A cigarette
He made rings
Of the smoke
He put the ashes
In the ash tray
Without talking to me
Without taking note
He stood up
He put
His hat on his head
He put on his raincoat
Because it was a rainy day
And he went away
Without a word
Without a glance aside
And me I laid
My head in my hand
And I cried.

Painstakingly the poet notes the trivia of coffee and cigarettes at the breakfast table, but he also notes the absence of something as routine as two lumps of sugar—conversation. We begin to sense the strain between the two people in the poem. When, even after donning hat and raincoat, the man gives no sign of recognizing the existence of his companion, we realize we are witnessing two people, probably two lovers, who can no longer communicate by word or glance, let alone touch. The series of

* Original French text of this translation appears on page 162.

insignificant, routine actions, listed in a maddening, metronomic rhyme scheme, increases the tension of suspense; the silences, the lacunae in the poem—or script—grow more menacing.

In the last line of the poem the tension breaks, the tears flow. Despite the matter-of-fact, almost curt phrasing, the emotion is quite credible. The poem provides an "objective correlative" sufficient to warrant the outburst of grief at the end. The surprise is that this emotion is transmitted not by eloquent rhetoric but by a set of astute stage directions.

The cinematic quality of a poem like *Déjeuner du matin* derives both from its lucid, terse, objective language and from its far-from-objective choice and order of images. The sequence of images, however, is still that of a "realistic" film strip; events occur in chronological order, and are limited to one stage setting.

But if we recall Picon's terms *montage* and *découpage*, and if we are familiar with Surrealist films which play tricks with a camera, we realize that the cinema influence on Prévert may extend to his other styles as well. Queval associates the poet's "spontaneous writing," more calculated than the automatism of the Surrealists, with the "camera that the author has in his head."[50] The critic is perhaps thinking of the inventory technique, which could certainly be compared to a capriciously spliced film. One might also consider *contre-pied* as a sort of double exposure, in which two apparently unrelated scenes are confounded. The tiger appears crouched in a cathedral pew, and a nun paces behind the bars of a cage (*Un tigre de Saint Vincent-de-Paul et une petite soeur de Bengale*). Are not the implications the same? Yet, obviously, as in the cited documentary, the poet betrays his feelings toward his material in the cutting and pasting of it. As Queval notes, the poet's method may change; his attitude never.[51]

Hence the camera style of Prévert, if we understand by the term a concentration on visual images of fine detail and a dramatic development of themes, pervades a great deal of his work. Both in the harsh realism of *La Grasse Matinée* and in the flights of intoxicated imagination of *La Lanterne magique de Picasso* the poet maintains his sense of spectacle. The former work is a newsreel; the latter is a circus. Queval compares Prévert's simple themes and character types with a puppet show, and the biting

satire of Daumier's drawings has a parallel in such Prévert car-
toons as *Le Grand Homme* (*Paroles,* 190) and *Le Droit Chemin.*

The Chorus

In all his many voices, though they may sound an echo among
ancient lyricists and modern Surrealists, Prévert guards his
originality. He draws music from everyday speech and twists
the most pedestrian proverbs into lines of unexpected humor or
emotional power. Mocking his very words, he puns, plays with
sounds, and rhymes incessantly, as a child prates. But he can
also write with deceptively simple grace. Léon Gros remarks
that this poet who will one day be held as the only true satirist of
the present period is also "the tenderest of elegiac poets and the
most impassioned partisan of that 'ardent reason' that Apollinaire
esteemed."[52]

But variety alone cannot explain Prévert's uniqueness. As
Picon says, "the poetry is in the pacing (*démarche*)." And the
démarche, the "gait" of the style, is a quality hard to assess. It
is certainly not merely a matter of rhythm. The flow of Prévert's
verse is often the flow of speech, and in his "delivery" the poet
shows genius. Timing can make the difference between a cheap
wisecrack and an incandescent witticism, and Prévert manifests
an excellent sense of timing in the structure, the *découpage,* of
his poems.

The conviction persists, difficult to sustain empirically, that
the value as well as the originality of Prévert's style depends on
his ability to combine the commonest words and expressions into
new patterns which effectively tap the reader's emotions. It is
Prévert the editor, arranging and splicing phrases and scraps of
phrases transcribed accurately from everyday speech, who is
most truly a poet. Without concerning himself with the word
recherché, the Latin and Greek residue in modern tongues, or
the subtleties of formal verse patterns, Prévert has concentrated
on translating all kinds of emotions into carefully ordered series
of notations, either sketching actions or exactly registering
spoken idiom; the action or speech and its position in a series
become more important than any properties of the symbols of

notation. The "poem" tries to disappear or to become clear as a camera lens, so that only gesture and utterance remain, charged, in context, with all the explosive significance of drama.

But no one style, even that of the camera, wholly accounts for Prévert's reputation; and perhaps no general commentary can unite into harmonious chorus his many voices. Gaudin's summary, apt as any, ends by saying simply that the genius of Prévert lies in the apparent nonchalance of his artistry.

Thus Prévert's poetry is formed of very diverse elements: social satire, a horror of metaphysics, a love of life, a fantasy optimistic for the most part, black humor. Nevertheless it is not in variety alone that the poet's originality abides, but also in the art by which, without appearing to bind himself to literary preoccupations, he knows how to translate sensations into words.[53]

CHAPTER 8

Old Men in Draughty Houses

Le monde mental
Ment
Monumentalement. —J.P.

The *cas Prévert* is both a reproach and a challenge to much American poetry and criticism.

Poems which are easily understood and both very popular and highly respected attack—at least implicitly—the position of those poet-critics who hold that modern poetry *must* be difficult and of very restricted appeal. On the other hand, among those few who have suspected all along that literature can have wide circulation and still be good, poetry like Prévert's ought to arouse a spark of revolutionary hope. To its handful of partisans in the English-speaking world, a book like *Paroles* seems to be just the remedy needed to combat a lingering complaint of modern literature: the hermeticism of poetry and a corresponding parochialism among critics.

So far, however, the poetry of Prévert and of those who write in a similar idiom has gone unnoticed in America. Some young poets read Prévert,[1] and one of the "Beat Generation" forefathers, Lawrence Ferlinghetti, has translated a portion of *Paroles* and copies Prévert's techniques in his own work;[2] but these authors have not themselves attained a reputation sufficient to stimulate a widespread study of the influences which formed their styles. One suspects, in fact, that the American literary Establishment would be as quick to condemn Prévert as it is to ridicule the "Beats."

The virtual neglect of not only Prévert but of most of the modern poets who write as he does, is itself a telling commentary on the bias of our orthodox criticism. Ironic it is, too, that reputable French critics have given Prévert respectful attention, even homage, but their American counterparts—while eagerly asserting the profound influence of French Symbolist theories on English and American poetry—ignore him for the most part. Yet Prévert in a certain sense grew out of that same Symbolist tradition.

I have said that prévertian poetry represents a challenge and a reproach to "modern" poetry and its handmaiden, the "New" Criticism. This is true for two reasons: (1) The obscurity, difficulty, and complexity of this modern poetry have been incorporated into dogma; obscurity, difficulty, and complexity are no longer neutral qualities of poetry in English; critics have proclaimed them necessary concomitants of it. (2) Inevitably, it seems, critics are driven to esteem these now-requisite qualities as virtues, so that they praise only poetry which possesses them; hence the current exaltation of the seventeenth-century metaphysical poets and the nineteenth-century Symbolists. What began as avant-garde fashion ends as esthetic theory.

To understand the devious means by which this prejudice in poetry and criticism has developed, it is necessary to define extensively that poetry which contemporary American critics label "modern." Once the nature of this poetry and the nature of the criticism which supports it are understood, it is easy to see the implied challenge of Prévert's work, which might not qualify in America either as "modern" or as good poetry.

There is, of course, more behind this challenge than one man's effort, for Prévert is only the latest exponent of one of the oldest and most vigorous currents in French poetry—*l'esprit gaulois*. And not all of contemporary American poetry is "modern"; some of it, a splinter from earlier movements or the sign of a new avant-garde, resembles the kind of poetry Prévert writes. But by comparing Prévert's work with orthodox "modern" American poetry, one may suggest that there is a fundamental difference between much recent poetry in France and its counterpart in America, a difference not only in manner, but in the whole concept of what poetry ought to do and how it ought to do it.

Name Dropping

"La poésie en Amérique aujourd'hui," stated the French comparatist René Taupin in 1929, "parle français."[3] Taupin based this epigram, a not-quite-absurd exaggeration, on an exhaustive study of American poetry from 1910 to 1920. Writing about this same decade and the following one, American critics inevitably mention the French influence on such major poets as Eliot, Pound, Crane, Williams, and Stevens. Almost any book on modern poetry devotes several pages to this influence, and at times it would seem more correct to say that American *criticism* now speaks French.

The same names are always mentioned: Baudelaire, Laforgue, Corbière, Mallarmé, Rimbaud, and sometimes even Verlaine and Gautier. Laforgue, since Eliot referred to him briefly, is probably the name most often dropped. Some critics treat this poet almost as if he were the principal forerunner of "modern" poetry, a conception that would undoubtedly strike most French critics as bizarre, to say the least.[4] Usually the combined influence of these nineteenth-century poets is loosely associated with the term "Symbolism," though that doctrine, or any other, is inadequate to encompass such diverse talents as Laforgue and Rimbaud, Verlaine and Mallarmé.

What, then, are modern American critics talking about when they refer to the "Symbolist" influence? To know this it is not necessary to analyze the formal accounts of the origins of the movement, its esthetic principles, and the kinds of poetry it produced. It is more important to examine the comments of critics in order to determine which of these principles and kinds of poetry exert an active influence on American poets. What Symbolism *is* will perhaps never be known; we are interested here in discovering what influential men of letters *think* it is.

A disgust for reality, one consistent theme of modern art, appeared around 1850 in the work of two men who early inspired the Symbolist movement. Baudelaire and Delacroix, working in different mediums, were aware of correspondences between their respective attitudes toward art. They agreed in their dissatisfaction with art that imitated nature.[5] Poetry and painting, in France, have for many years developed simultaneously along the same lines,[6] and this withdrawal from reality as perceived by the senses was from the beginning one of the most important of these lines of development.[7] In literature, the tendency eventually manifested itself in a preoccupation with the irrational qualities of experience, with the sound rather than the meaning of words, and, after the turn of the century, with the incoherent images of the unconscious.[8]

The germ of this kind of poetry can be traced back to the Romantic movement, in which the belief in inspiration or "non-intellectual intuition" roughly corresponds to this later reliance on the unconscious;[9] but, with Baudelaire, the fascination with the unconscious underwent an important modification.[10] In withdrawing from everyday reality, Baudelaire not only showed his preference for an artificial world created by the poetic imagination, he denounced the "real world." Modern art, especially the Dadaist and Surrealist movements, has continued to denounce it. Claude Vigée calls this nihilistic tradition, which he entitles "the poetry of exile from being," the "dominant force in modern literature."[11]

The retreat from reality, which Vigée sees as a form of escapism growing out of a basically nihilistic philosophy, culminated in the "pure" poetry of Mallarmé. At this point, two new important aspects of the Symbolist movement developed: Obscurity in poetry and the isolation of the poet. Rejecting reality involved rejecting common sense and the public interest as well.

From Mallarmé on, the Symbolists repeatedly expressed the belief that obscurity was a *desirable* quality in poetry and that the poet's role of pariah was a heroic one. Arthur Symons, in *The Symbolist Movement*, a book which one critic claims has "to a remarkable degree" formed the character of modern poetry,[12] praised the obscurity of Mallarmé's work. He even approved of that obscurity as a means of excluding most readers as unworthy.

But who, in our time has wrought so subtle a veil, shining on this side, where the few are, a thick cloud on the other, where are the many? The oracles have always had the wisdom to hide their secrets in the obscurity of many meanings, or of what has seemed meaningless; and might it not, after all, be the finest epitaph for a self-respecting man of letters to be able to say, even after the writing of many books: I have kept my secret, I have not betrayed myself to the multitude?[13]

The value of Mallarmé's poetry, Symons concludes, lies in its ability to imply rather than to state meanings, in its "capacity for allusion and suggestion."[14] This subtlety, or obscurity—the distinction depends upon which side of the veil one sees—denied the poet a large audience; only those with powers of intellect and imagination comparable to his own were capable of understanding him.

So Mallarmé withdrew to "icy solitude."[15] For him life was "the great enemy."[16] But even before his death he became a legend in the literary world; he was thought of as the lonely dreamer, a godlike figure in his own universe created by poetic magic, but ignored by his fellow men in the everyday world. Early in the twentieth century the doctrine of obscurity as a valued poetic quality gained force, and with it went the image, of which Mallarmé remains the prototype, of the artist as exiled demiurge.[17]

Ever since Symons' book introduced Mallarmé to England and America, critics have been discussing obscurity in poetry and the isolation of the artist. One need only remark the titles of some typical articles written during the last twenty years: "The American Literary Expatriate,"[18] "The Obscurity of the Poet,"[18a] "The Isolation of the American Artist,"[18b] "The Isolation of Modern Poetry,"[18c] "Are Poets Out of Touch with Life?"[18d] This unflagging discussion confirms one of the commonplaces of contemporary literary history: the influence of the mallarméan style of poetry has been especially powerful on English-speaking poets.

There is general agreement . . . that the modern idiom in poetry depends primarily on two traditions—the metaphysical, stemming from John Donne and his period, and the symbolist stemming from Mallarmé.[19]

The kinship between these traditions appears in their emphasis on the "subtlety of their descriptions of feelings," and in the "subsequent limitation of their audience."[20] "Subtlety," of course, becomes obscurity for those who do not understand, and the "limitation" of a poet's audience means his isolation from society. "It is the poet against society, society against the poet, a direct antagonism . . . ,"[21] Symons noted at the turn of the century, foreseeing the conflict, and nearly fifty years later a critic of modern poetry writes that "there has certainly never been an age when poetry has been so completely divorced from national life as it has been for the last twenty years."[22] The poet Archibald MacLeish and the literary historian Robert E. Spiller agree that the alienated artist is, at least in recent decades, a peculiarly American type. Of this type MacLeish says, "There are merely —or so it looks overseas—a number of more or less isolated individuals living quite out of the stream of American life on an island somewhere. . . ."[23] Spiller, tracing back to Poe the "image" of the poet in spiritual exile, believes the Symbolist movement merely "fell into this tradition."[24] Whether or not American literature furnishes the archetypal pattern, American poets and critics provide the clearest examples of what may indeed be a world-wide condition: the isolation of artists and their work from the general public. Of the period between the World Wars, F. O. Matthiessen writes, "American poetry in these years furnished the most serious evidence of a cleavage between what we have learned to call mass civilization and minority culture."[25]

The immediate descendants of French Symbolism accepted this condition of isolation as their "natural status."[26] No longer concerned with instructing or amusing the public, they indulged in private experiments to purify their art, to purge it of any direct, didactic content, and to make of it the source of subtle, impersonal, "poetic" emotions rather than the record of the poet's own human ones. This sort of poetry, designed to live "alone, by itself, and for itself,"[27] had to depend on the refined sensibility of the reader for its ultimate value. The "poetic emotion" in Mallarmé's work, for example, could be tapped only by means of a *creative* effort on the part of the reader, whose enjoyment stemmed from a penetrating of deliberate obscurity.

. . . (the poetic emotion) can occur in the reader's soul only through an act of creation parallel to that which the poet has already performed, only through the joy of difficulty overcome and an obscurity which gradually grows clear.[28]

The aspects of Symbolist theory we wish to emphasize here are now clear. (1) Withdrawing from any contact with everyday reality, the poet as poet also rejects human life itself in so far as this life connotes a social process. The poet's familiar personality vanishes. His poems are mystic charms which invoke experiences or states of mind which transcend ordinary consciousness. (2) These charms are *necessarily* obscure. Fifteen years after Mallarmé's death in 1895, "the attraction of mystery was progressively increasing . . . and . . . a belief in the particular efficacy of poetic experience in this respect was spreading."[29] And Raymond admits that obscurity is an "indispensable element" in the poetics of Paul Valéry, the most devoted exponent of Mallarmé's method.[30] (3) Denying the value for poetry of everyday human emotions, believing in the superior efficacy of obscure language as the key to occult mysteries, the poet places himself in isolation. Only those whose intellect and sensibility match his own can penetrate, and in penetrating enjoy, the labyrinth of his poetic imagination.

The American—and English—poet who absorbed these aspects of French Symbolism and passed them on to succeeding generations was of course T. S. Eliot.

. . . the most influential poet of his time, Eliot sent the younger men on the ways that he had travelled. As he had explored, among others, the divergent roads taken by the symbolists, so, following him, did his contemporaries and his juniors.[31]

Although many other major American poets of Eliot's generation, Wallace Stevens and Ezra Pound for example, have perhaps been equally influenced by French poetry,[32] it is Eliot who, in his criticism, clearly formulated the Symbolist doctrine of "modern" American poetry.

The nihilistic tendency of Symbolism, which Vigée also called the "dominant force in modern literature," certainly appears in *The Waste Land*. And this horrified disgust at the modern world, the first stage of withdrawal, is expressed impersonally. "In the realm of Eliot's poetry," says Deutsch, "the vision is known only as it recedes. . . ."[33] for the poet has "objectified his private responses to a sordid and tawdry society."[34] As a result,

The Waste Land and the poems which immediately succeed it
are "completely depersonalized."[35]

Supplementing his practice with theory, Eliot himself has
written that the poet's art is "a continual extinction of personality,"[36] in which private emotions figure not at all.

Poetry is not a turning loose of emotion, but an escape from emotion; it is not the expression of personality, but an escape from
personality.[37]

Eventually, however, Eliot escaped, not into a mystic realm created out of poetic symbols, but into the past—into the medieval
mysticism of the orthodox Church. Still, Eliot's poetry is rela-
tively "pure" in that it deals with generalized rather than personal emotions. Although we may sense a worshipful attitude
toward history and tradition, and abhorrence of the Sweeneys
and Bleisteins of the world, Eliot's style ordinarily lacks the
vehemence of the personal lyric.

In perfect accord with the "full, lively, and continually growing modern esthetic movement" of Symbolism,[38] Eliot found it
necessary to be obscure in the expression of his impersonal
mysticism.

We can only say that it appears likely that poets in our civilization,
as it exists at present, must be *difficult*. . . . The poet must become
more and more comprehensive, more allusive, more indirect, in order
to force, to dislocate if necessary, language into his meaning.[39]

We shall now see how American and English critics after Eliot
have digested his remarks and made of them a rigid, esthetic
principle of "modern" poetry.

The "profound influence" of the French Symbolists, says
Elizabeth Drew, operating through the "channel" of Eliot and
Pound, is responsible for the "oblique approach" of today's
poetry.[40] Mallarmé's doctrine of "indirectness" or "suggestiveness," derived ultimately from Poe, seems in fact to be the aspect
of Symbolism which has been stressed the most by contemporary
criticism. "Suggestive indefiniteness" and "conscious craftsmanship," claims J. Isaacs, are "the whole method of Mallarmé to
which all our modern poets are indebted directly or indirectly."[41]

And Louise Bogan, one of Eliot's most enthusiastic admirers, talks of his "modern sensibility," French inspired, which achieves "intense feeling by oblique means."[42]

These critics, Eliot included, ostensibly avoid the term "obscurity," preferring to substitute the euphemisms "indirectness," "difficulty," "suggestiveness," "obliqueness," or some combination of these terms. Others, perhaps recalling the somewhat embarrassing notes Eliot affixed to *The Waste Land* in order to explain the poem, try to defend the application of the more troublesome word. Often the critic's strategy is to stretch it to cover all poetry.

We shall not be able to judge fairly the more extreme instances of symbolist method unless we are perfectly clear on this point: that privacy and obscurity, to some degree, are inevitable in all poetry.[43]

Ever since Coleridge began to speculate about the poetic imagination, and more particularly in the past fifty years, poets have discovered increasingly elaborate reasons for believing that poetry must be shrouded in darkness.[44]

And yet it is not just modern poetry, but poetry, that is today obscure.[45]

William Van O'Connor justifies modern poetry, possibly "more obscure than any other [poetry] in English literature," on essentially the same grounds, arguing that "the nature of poetic language invites obscurity."[46]

From an originally defensive position, a few critics shift to a firm faith in the superior value of the unclear. Unable to ignore the charge of obscurity, or to regard it as a necessary evil, these critics have chosen to call it a definite virtue.

An affirmation of obscurity in poetry must force on us a reconsideration of the function of language. Obscurity in poetry cannot be regarded as merely a negative quality, a failure to attain a state of perfect clarity. It is a positive value, but more, it is a whole series of such values.[47]

Poetry which thus faithfully obeys the law of its nature is bound at times to be obscure; and to complain of this is like bemoaning the wetness of water or the hardness of stone. We should rather honour the poet who, sooner than falsify his vision, has the courage and perception to embrace obscurity.[48]

We have now reached a stage where people can assert that complexity, subtlety, and ambiguity are in themselves signs of good poetry. . . .[49]

Comments such as these suggest that Eliot and his successors have sired a school of apologists for the type of poetry they write.

Two critical approaches seem to have evolved out of the appraisal of "Symbolist" poetics. The least important of these is Herbert Read's position that the "emotional unity which is the *raison d'être* of every poem cannot be measured by the instruments of reason. . . . The poem must be received directly, without questioning, and loved or hated."[50] Such extreme impressionism would, of course, endanger all criticism in its role of explicator; the critic could at best tell us only what he likes and dislikes. Given the belief that obscurity is a "positive value," Read has no alternative but to contend that criticism has no business explaining away that obscurity.

The other type of criticism, the major one in the twentieth century, is the "New" Criticism fostered by I. A. Richards.[51] Through the use of the vocabulary and techniques of psychology and semantic analysis, Richards set the precedent for elucidating the "meaning" of poetry by applying to it scientific methods of inquiry. The development of scientific method, according to Stanley Edgar Hyman, is "one of the principal implications of modern criticism."[52] Another chronicler of modern criticism, Walter Sutton, remarks, "A concern for scientific method and discipline can be seen in the psychological criticism of the 1920's, the sociological criticism of the Thirties, and the New Criticism of the 1940's and 1950's."[53]

Symbiosis

It is easy to see the relationship, which was established almost immediately, between the poetic doctrine of obscurity, and the critical doctrine of logical, scientific explication. If the poet strove to obtain *absolute* obscurity, the utterly hermetic poem

[114]

inaccessible to the intellect and affective only for the "privileged reader"[54] with a "metaphysical sensibility"[55] as refined as the poet's, he would reduce the critic to puzzled silence or an approving nod. The critic, in short, would be out of a job.

Even the pure poets, however, had no intention of isolating themselves to such an extent. Eliot, and a number of poets after him, built a critical doctrine which would fit "modern" poetry. Eliot's first move to bring about this accord was an evasive maneuver; he insisted on the value of "tradition,"[56] which allowed him to pay as little attention as possible to recent poetry and the problem of obscurity. The mention of a few nineteenth-century French poets and his homage to Pound excepted, Eliot is silent on the subject of the poetry of his own time—including his own. He stipulates only that new English poetry must somehow extend the tradition of English literature. Even the French Symbolists are discussed only in relation to the English metaphysical poets, for they are, Eliot says, "nearer" the school of Donne than any modern English poet.[57] The effect of this vague *rapprochement* was a modification of the Symbolist poetic which was extremely important to the future of criticism.

The seventeenth-century metaphysical poets were not obscure in the same way Mallarmé was. They were, rather, difficult: their poetry was cerebral, a poetry of "wit," and therefore accessible to reason. Confusing Symbolist obscurity with metaphysical difficulty allowed Eliot to speak of the difficulty or complexity of modern poetry and imply at the same time that this poetry contained a logical, ordered substructure never beyond the apprehension of the critical intellect.

"Order" is the key concept here. It is the basis of Eliot's modern "classicism," rooted in the past,[58] and the necessary assumption of any explanatory criticism. For Eliot, "the function of traditional criticism . . . is the establishment of order, and the enemy is disorder."[59] This principle, that the study of phenomena leads to the discovery of intelligible patterns in the universe, is axiomatic to all science;[60] and if criticism was to be a science it had to adopt this axiom.

Thus I. A. Richards, equipped with the theories of modern psychology, proceeded to outline the methods by which the "obscurity" of poetry, often stemming since Baudelaire from a dependence on the unconscious mind for both material and form, could be explained away. He assumed, in taking this path, that the work of the poet, "is the ordering of what in most minds is disordered."[61] The relation of criticism to modern poetry became something like that between a physicist and a swami. The swami enchants us briefly by causing the crystal ball to glow magically and to give indirect clues to the mystery of life; then the physicist flicks on the lights and proves that it was all only mirrors and electricity, quite comprehensible after all. To describe the scientific bias of contemporary critics, Stephen Spender elaborates a metaphor similarly drawn from the technological world.

Criticism makes such high claims today that sometimes one may be misled into concluding that the purpose of a poem is to provide material for critical analysis, and that we understand no work of art unless there is a radiologist who throws an X-ray photograph of the skeleton and organs of the poem on to a ground-glass screen at the very moment when the reader is reading it.[62]

Critics of course would deny that their role is so unromantic. Richards himself says of Eliot's poetry that "the items are united by the accord, contrast, and interaction of their emotional effects, not by an intellectual scheme that analysis must work out."[63] Yet his criticism is obviously the attempt to find just such a scheme in poetry, or to impose one on it. The very words "accord," "contrast," "interaction," and "items" that are "united" suggest a system, or pattern, of relationships.

It comes as something of a surprise, then, to learn that most of the accounts of the New Criticism assign to this movement a special function beyond, or outside of, the scope of science, if not one directly opposed to it. A central belief of this school of criticism, asserts William J. Handy, is that "the special symbolic formulation of language which characterizes the literary work is unique in its ability to represent a part of man's experience that cannot be represented adequately by the abstractions of logic."[64] And the critic, it is implied, is concerned primarily with this "special symbolic formulation." Yet, again and again, the modern critic stresses the *analytic* character of his effort:

The characteristic common to all these latter critics [John Crowe Ransom, William Empson, Eliot, Richards, Yvor Winters] is intensive analysis of the literary work. A designation more useful than "new criticism" would be "analytical criticism."[65]

Ransom himself has written

Many critics today are writing analytically and with close intelligence, in whatever terms, about the logical substance or structure of the poem, and its increment of irrelevant local substance or texture.[66]

There is something mechanistic, too, about Spiller's observation that "the new analytical criticism supplies a 'job of work' to be done and the tools, mainly of rhetoric, with which to do it."[67] Surely criticism devoted so passionately to a close study of the details of a text has much in common with empirical science, however strongly some literary theorists claim the contrary.

The ambivalence of New Criticism with regard to science may be responsible for the "maze of incompatible assumptions"[68] that Murray Krieger finds among the leading proponents of this school. Irving Howe describes the internal conflict as one between the critic's theory, which obliges him to be a dispassionate technician of literary analysis, and his experience, which encourages him to be a passionate moral philosopher. Such critics, Howe says, mix "close analyses of texts with oracular pronouncements of a sort that might be called moralistic impressionism."[69] Most observers feel, however, that the preoccupation with analysis overrides moral concerns in much modern criticism.

The French Symbolists, on the other hand, have never agreed on the function of the intellect in poetry. Baudelaire found in Poe the idea of "conscious poetic manipulation as opposed to poetic inspiration."[70] But Mallarmé, concentrating on the music rather than the logic of language, and Rimbaud, in whom the "poetic sense becomes closely akin to the mystical or prophetic sense,"[71] both seem to believe that truly pure poetry originates from a source beyond the intellect.

To allow criticism a place in modern poetry, it was necessary to reconcile these two contradictory conceptions of the poetic faculty in such a way that at least the critic of poetry, if not its creator, could find in it a principle of order. Richards, admitting that the artist himself is often not in the least concerned with communication, maintains that communication is nevertheless the principal aim of art. The basis of communication is, of course, a system of ordered symbols. The critic must give an "account of communication"; that is, he must find and record the patterning of experience, the order in a poem which constitutes its meaning or "main purpose."[72] When the critic is successful in his elucidation, "the artist is entirely justified in his apparent neglect of the main purpose of his work."[73] Thus the poet and critic can co-exist, working autonomously; the one expressing he knows not quite what from he knows not quite where, the other explaining just what it is the artist is communicating, whether he knows it or not, and from what nook in his psyche he got it.

Hybrids

Most poets, however, were perfectly capable of scientific criticism themselves; they could learn from critics what they were supposed to be doing and repeat the process *consciously*. So the poet-critic was born. The kind of work produced by this hybrid, as influential in criticism as in poetry[74]—if indeed these activities are separable in this type—was highly complex, but deliberately made subject to analysis.

. . . the Eliot poem demands cerebration if it is to be understood. This is what differentiates Eliot from the French Symbolists who so influenced him. . . . Eliot's poetry has all the suggestiveness of the French Symbolists, but it has a much more complex kind of organization than their poetry has, and, further, the suggestiveness manifests itself only to the alert intellect.[75]

For the too-obvious logical structure of traditional metaphysical poetry, the modern poet substituted a "psychological process," a "kind of cerebral and emotional shorthand."[76] This shorthand turns out to be fully as "logical," under analysis, as the old philosophic longhand.

The talented Americans of Eliot's generation, says Bogan, "shared an impulse toward emotional veracity and intellectual analysis,"[77] and critical works of the age "brought the sharpest sort of rational analytical method to bear on the poetic expression of the symbolic and the irrational."[78] The critic fails to add that such poetic expression is no longer spontaneously symbolic and irrational after the "sharpest sort of rational analytical method" is through with it.

The eventual effect of the Symbolist influence was thus a powerful movement toward intellectualism in criticism, first, and then in poetry itself. New Criticism, one of its foremost advocates states, attacks the notion that "the work of art deals immediately with the passions, instead of mediately," and affirms that "art is among the highly reflective or cognitive activities, not recognizable when cited for its effectiveness as a mode of passion."[79] This is Eliot's theory of the "poetic emotion" as derived from Mallarmé, with the added corollary that this emotion is constructed by the intellect.

The chain of development is now complete. Symbolist poetry was by its very nature obscure; Symbolist criticism made of that obscurity a virtue; then, to justify its existence, criticism had to formulate a "new" method which could reduce that obscurity to order, to "communication."

It is hardly too much to say that the Symbolist movement was not only the cause of many of the varieties of modern obscurity, but also of the critical techniques that have been evolved in order that such poetry may be inoffensively discussed. . . .[80]

Finally, the poet, seeing this process in action, learns how to manipulate the mirrors and electric wires that produce poetic "magic," aware that the physicist (perhaps himself) will find them, but anxious to let it be known that he, too, as a poet, knows where they are and how they work.

We now see that the modern poetic universe is composed of an impersonal, apparently obscure, highly intellectual poetry and a scientific, expository criticism. The two maintain a harmonious, symbiotic relationship. The denizens of this universe are their own audience, "a small but infinitely eager and educable audience," formed through the "interplay between originality in writing and a criticism founded on fresh attitudes."[81]

Modern criticism forms, so to speak, the crystal shell and support of this universe, and there are two alarming cracks to be discerned in that shell. The most obvious one occurs when the scientific critic recognizes that he must make value judgments. Richards agrees that one of the two pillars of any critical theory is "an account of value" (the other is of course the "account of communication"), which is precisely the sort of judgment no science ever attempts to make. As Hyman points out, the nature of literature makes it imperative that the critic enter "a purely subjective area,"[82] or his analysis, no matter how scientifically valid, is worthless. The second shortcoming of modern criticism is that, excluding the poet's attempts at self-fulfillment, there is no clear notion of the relationship of the artist to his readers.

The modern critic no longer makes the "two principal assumptions about literature in the past," that it is "essentially a type of moral instruction, and that it is essentially a type of entertainment and amusement."[83] The poet merely writes obscure poetry, assumed to be good partly because it is obscure, and the critic explains what the poetry actually means. But the vital question is: To whom is he explaining it? And if it is neither instructive nor amusing, why does he bother with it at all?

The poet, too, appears to be troubled by the effects of his excessively intellectual pursuits and the separation from the public which devotion to "modern" poetry entails. Eliot himself predicts that "[an] extreme awareness and concern for language . . . is something which ultimately must break down, owing to an increasing strain, against which the human mind and nerves will rebel." And even critics with an established position in the hierarchy of the poetic universe suggest that modern poetry's "tendency toward expertness of control . . . is accompanied by a complete exhaustion of experimentation . . ." and a "diminution of creative vitality," or "drying out of emotion."[84]

An Alternative

One way to see clearly this quandary of modern American poetry and criticism is to contrast it with the work of Prévert, who exemplifies an entirely different approach to poetry, yet who came out of the very cultural and intellectual environment which harbored the Symbolist movement. To understand the phenomenon of Prévert, however, it is first necessary to consider the stages of development through which French poetry has passed in the last half century.

After Mallarmé had incorporated the principle of obscurity into poetry, and with it the role of the poet as exiled hero, artists in the first two decades of the twentieth century pushed his doctrine to a radical extreme. Dada and its more successful offspring, Surrealism, attained ultimate obscurity in the form of chaos and nonsense. "The extreme of obscurity," Dada was the point of no return for a tendency that had been growing for half a century.[85]

Surrealism, however, reaffirmed the Symbolists' faith in the value of the unconscious as a source of the poetic image. This faith, in fact, became central to the new poetic theory. And, like the Symbolists, Surrealist poets detested the realities of modern civilization.[86] But the reaction of the Surrealist writers was not one of withdrawal, but one of attack. They set about destroying in order to gain access to a new "super-reality."

This "higher Reality beyond the pale of our everyday experience"[87] was, as in the case of Baudelaire, to be uncovered in the unsounded depths of psychic life. But along with the exploration of inner worlds, the Surrealists strove actively to change the outer one; they denounced traditional bourgeois art, and they allied themselves with Communist aims. Thus in at least two important ways the Surrealists and Dadaists departed from Symbolist theory: (1) They subordinated craftsmanship in poetry to other ends; i.e., the transcendence of ordinary consciousness in the individual, the destruction of accepted standards of "literature" and beauty;[88] and (2) they consecrated the principle of revolt, both artistic and political, in poetry.

Thibaudet distinguishes three types of revolt in the Symbolist movement: (1) Stylistic revolt, inherent in the development of vers libre; (2) the esthetic revolt of the doctrines of "pure" poetry; and (3) the idea of revolution itself.[89] Surrealism continued only the first and third types of revolution, while for a new generation of Symbolist poets, of whom Valéry was the most famous, the esthetics of pure poetry crystallized into dogma. Symbolist revolt, in this case, became Symbolist tradition.

Valéry, the last of the major Symbolist poets, had a career remarkably like Eliot's. But while Eliot began a tradition of impersonal, obscure poetry with an accompanying intellectual criticism, Valéry was the last important flowering of that tradition in France. Valéry's reputation, like Eliot's, rests on a small body of poetry and an extensive, complex criticism, the two being almost inseparable. And Valéry, too, assumed the function of explaining poetry to a select coterie of admirers.[90]

Furthermore, Valéry continued the mallarméan tradition of the poet, exiled "because of his opposition to the main stream,"[91] who refuses to flatter vulgar taste. He thought of the poet as a *froid savant*, and his own work, again parallel to Eliot's, assigned the intellect to a central position in the process of artistic creation. In fact, for Valéry, art was more "analysis," premeditated "construction," and "calculation" than "creation."[92]

And finally, like most Symbolists, Valéry preferred poetry to life, esthetic response to human emotion. In a "mandarin" language that was wholly literary[93] he sought "the pure point of absolute contempt and the perfect vacuity of the consciousness that rejects life."[94] One recalls the definition of poetry as an "escape from emotion."

The type of poetry Valéry advocated, so rigorously pure it was nearly a religion,[95] won critical acclaim, but few readers other than the specially trained literary man. Indeed, Maulnier proclaimed that for such poetry any contact with the French public was almost "insupportable."[96] But critical acclaim, as the recent history of French literature shows, was not enough to maintain the prominence of "pure" poetry. A new kind of art, with tenets almost wholly antagonistic to the old Symbolist tradition, gathered strength throughout the first four decades of the twentieth century and at last broke down the barrier between the poet and the people.

Rebellion

Perhaps the most lively quality of much of the new poetry was its spirit of revolt. Continual revolt is exactly what made it always "new." Out of Symbolism the Cubist, Dadaist, and Surrealist schools took the bold energy of iconoclasm—and very little else. Of revolt itself, however, they made a tradition.

The symbolist revolution, the last so far, will perhaps turn out to have been the last altogether, because it incorporated the idea of chronic revolution into the normal condition of literature.[97]

George Lemaître, tracing the backgrounds of Cubism in literature, finds the origin of the twentieth-century revolt in the Romanticism of Rousseau, who stressed the validity of intuition and sentiment,[98] issuing the first "challenge to the hegemony of rationalism in France."[99] Other critics consider Rimbaud, possessed by "the demon of revolt and destruction," a prototype of the modern avant-garde poet.[100] And some, like Brodin and the historian Clouard, feel that the first important surge of revolt came with Dada, after World War I. Clouard suggests that this sudden rioting of the young may have exploded because of the dry and sterile artificiality of Valéry's sort of orthodox symbolism.[101] In any event a "tradition of iconoclasts" was founded.[102]

And Prévert, to be sure, is a member of that tradition above all others. In the previous chapter, his political inclinations were noted. Like those of the Surrealists, they are revolutionary, associating Prévert with the whole recent Marxist movement in French literature.[103] The destructive tendency of the Surrealist movement, already discussed in its stylistic implications, appeared in the form of "virulent satire."[104]

Prévert's reputation rests to a great extent on the aptness and acidity of his satire, satire often brutal in its directness, and totally unlike the world-weary, impersonal poetry of Valéry and Eliot. Prévert attacks, as we have seen, the Church and the authority of the state—the very institutions the Anglo-Catholic Eliot upheld. He is also violently anti-intellectual, placing his faith in the honest but dumb emotions of the Sweeneys of the world.

The tradition of revolt culminating in Prévert is one of *total* revolt.

. . . political, intellectual, social revolt. Revolt against the "bourgeois" parliamentary regime, evident in the adherence of many youths to maurrassism or to communism. . . . Revolt finally against traditional literary language, against which an ordered offensive is beginning. . . .[105]

This last revolt, however, is the really important one in recent French literature: it is the rejection of the literary or "mandarin" language of Symbolism and a return to the idiom of common speech. The term "anti-poetry," applied to Prévert's work, is quite accurate if we mean by poetry "pure" or mallarméan poetry and its doctrine of "poetic" emotion, obscurity, and the isolation of the artist.

Apollinaire and Max Jacob began the "wholly new" poetic style,[106] which drew on journalistic jargon, slang, and popular song. Such writers refused to make of their art a "système clos," and sought inspiration not only in deliberate cultivation or exacerbation of the individual's subconscious, but also in life as a communal process. Their language was correspondingly a living language, "plus libre, brusque, jaillissant. . . ."[107]

For one thing, the new poetic language did not concentrate on the marvel of itself. It strove to purge itself of the literary.[108] In reaction against the Classicism of Valéry, Claudel, and Gide, for whom beauty of style was the ultimate beauty, modern French literature, *littérature engagée*, uses language "with some impatience and even with some mistrust."[109]

. . . these *serious* men (Sartre, Salacrou, Prévert) show a tendency to reject literature, to forbid themselves to write it.[110]

In place of "literary" literature and "poetic" poetry, Prévert gives us *Paroles*. He writes of the emotions of everyday life: the suffering of the poor, the anger of the oppressed, the joy of love, the wonder of a child. And there is, above all, no obscurity in what he says. He often tries, in fact, to communicate at an elemental—not a subconscious—level, so that sensations and emotions have a direct impact on the reader, striking him before he is conscious of any verbal abstraction.

The widespread appeal of this direct, colloquial style is now a fact of history, though very recent and still unfinished history. Prévert, by writing of the feelings of Sweeney in his own tongue, has brought poetry to him and received an enthusiastic welcome. He has done what Maulnier thought impossible; he has been read, heard, seen, and applauded by the general public.

The Challenge

This, then, is the challenge of Prévert to "modern" American poetry and criticism: he writes personal, nonintellectual, popular poetry, and no criticism at all; he views contemporary civilization not as a wasteland, but as a battleground where real, red blood must be spilled to right injustice; and the last thing in the world he wants to do is "escape from emotion." Further, he is no exile. Behind the prototype who appears throughout his poetry, "le pauvre bougre," appears the horde of the proletariat.[111] Prévert is their willing spokesman, the enemy of all Prufrocks.

Based on the excellence of obscurity and the necessity for the isolation of the artist, the canon of orthodox American criticism must either alter its position or condemn such poetry. The latter course would involve making a value judgment, something modern criticism, safe in "tradition," shies from, whereas the first would require a radically modified set of critical standards. Indeed, Richards foresaw at the end of the first quarter of the twentieth century that the artist's predicament could not remain static. He predicted that the separation of art and life, the poet and society, would grow sharper.

With the increase of population the problem presented by the gulf between what is preferred by the majority and what is accepted as excellent by the most qualified opinion has become infinitely more serious and appears likely to become threatening in the near future.[112]

The New Critics, judging themselves qualified to know what was excellent, could not, however, inhibit the public, and even certain poets, from preferring whatever they wished; by mid-century there were more and more dissenters from "modern" poetry and "scientific" criticism.[113] Some critics were nevertheless so blinded by their training in the Symbolist tradition that even after 1950 Wallace Fowlie could claim that "the lesson taught by Mallarmé that there is no such thing as immediate poetry" was "the central legacy of modern [French?] poetry."[114] Such a statement seems to ignore a major movement of French literature since the end of World War I, though it does indeed apply to "modern" *American* poetry and criticism. It is worth remarking that Fowlie has more recently referred to *Surrealism* as "the strongest collective movement French art has ever known."[115] Still, this critic finds a quasi-mystical character in the Surrealists, who, he says, write an "ascetic language," and whose poetry is "the experience of language, and not the experience of sentiment."[116] Also, "their kind of poetry has its sources in Nerval, in an art that is *difficult*."[117] (Italics mine.) Fowlie has a few kind words for Prévert, mitigated by an allusion to the "dangerously facile," but dismisses him from the ranks of the "pure" Surrealist poets.[118] Again one suspects that the biases of American criticism, especially when that criticism focuses on "modern" poetry, inhibit a fair estimate of writers like Prévert.

Off-Beats

Actually, American poetry in the twentieth century was not all "modern." Masters, Lindsay, and Sandburg wrote frankly proletarian literature in more or less colloquial language.[119] They were mild revolutionaries compared to the Surrealists, but they stood diametrically opposed to the reactionary Eliot doctrine upholding traditions in politics, religion, and literature. They foreshadowed a brief uprising in the 1930's of leftist poetry: Horace Gregory, Muriel Rukeyser, Max Eastman, and Kenneth Fearing were then the most notable rebels, but the movement died out before the end of World War II.[120]

Surrealism itself had almost no direct effect on American literature.[121] The device of relating images according to instinctive association rather than logical pattern and the dependence on the unconscious as a source of poetic material appeared in modern American poetry stripped of their magic and their revolutionary implications. Critics turned the search for inspiration from the unconscious into an analytical method, by which the unconscious, implicit and irrational was immediately made conscious, explicit and rational. The poet became a harmless puzzle-maker; the critic an equally harmless puzzle-solver.[122]

In England, Dylan Thomas and the early W. H. Auden succeeded in departing from the mainstream of Symbolist poetry. Auden wrote in protest against bourgeois capitalism, and his language was often direct to the point of at least suggesting social action. But seldom have new poets followed his example, perhaps, as Frank Kermode suggests, (borrowing from Keats) because "we still cannot bear poetry which has a design upon us."[123] Thomas was a genius but not always a self-aware one; consequently, the critics were not sure of his intentions either. His sort of obscurity was genuine, and though his poetry was pleasing and popular, and influenced younger writers, critics tended merely to applaud it and hurry on, because they did not quite understand how "The Long-Legged Bait" fit into English literary tradition, and because they were perhaps at a loss to know how to bring scientific criticism to bear on such poetry.

The proletarian American poets, and even the poets of the "Beat Generation," who resemble the Dadaists of forty years before in their taste for iconoclasm, obscenities, and zany humor, have something in common with Prévert: they have a great enthusiasm for the life of the senses and fundamental human emotions; they revolt against conventional society and literary taste; they write in a rich, imagistic, but colloquial style. They are either forerunners or members of the group of "genuine avant-garde poets of the 1950's," who, Vigée believes, are "breaking away from the century-old and played-out, symbol-ridden, indirect, often inhuman poetry of nihilism. . . ."[124] It is this kind of American poetry which is yet ignored; it is the American tradition to which, says Hyman, Eliot "seems almost entirely blind . . . if not in flight from it."[125]

Dissenters point out that the intellectual and impersonal qualities of "modern" poetry have isolated the artist from part of himself. His human emotions have no contact with his poetic ones, and ". . . the straightforward lyric of simple, direct intensity of thought and feeling is very rare."[126] Such lyrics are rare, perhaps, because the one-sidedness of modern poetry eventually leads to the atrophy not only of individual minds, but even of their vehicle of expression—the literary magazine.

. . . the literary atmosphere for the reception of any deep-springing art, advance-guard or otherwise, is miserable. Certainly the literary reviews have never been so poor in forty years in this country. In the interests of a secure academism . . . they print nothing that is arresting.[127]

Most of our contemporary poets are writing out into a climate of poetic officialdom or pre-tested approval, based largely on the principles which the New Criticism has espoused, and on the opinions of those who count in modern letters. We have lost all sense of personal intimacy between the poet and his reader. . . .[128]

Thus, what sources are available to the poet, being conditioned to the appreciation of obscure, impersonal, highly allusive poems, present him with little opportunity to break out of the cycle.

The principal fault which the *cas Prévert* illuminates in "modern" American poetry is simply that this poetry is governing and at the same time governed by a criticism that evades the most vital question in art: how to make value judgments. If criticism no longer assumes that literature functions as a means of either moral instruction or entertainment, it substitutes for these traditional functions no new ones for which a substantial value can be determined. In a scathing reproach to Eliot and his admirers, Karl Shapiro hints that modern criticism has deliberately withdrawn from the responsibility of passing judgment on literature.

The strategic purpose of Eliot's criticism was to prevent judgment; that is the purpose of the criticism which he gave birth to (called the New Criticism), to replace judgment by theory.[129]

The English critic Graham Hough makes a similar charge:

The best modern criticism has made surprisingly little attempt to judge the most challenging contemporary literature, to estimate its value, or what can amount to the same thing, to place it properly in relation to the literature of the past.[130]

This criticism, assuming on no valid grounds the value of "indirectness," "impersonality," and the lack of all emotion but the artificial, rarefied sort, is of course unlikely to esteem Prévert very highly. In his outspoken stand against social injustice, and in his taste for biting satire and slapstick comedy, the French poet is openly a moralist, decidedly a humorist.

"Modern" American poetry and criticism, if they are to absorb poetry of the kind Prévert writes, must examine and re-evaluate themselves and each other. The process has already begun—

new critics are attacking New Critics. It is doubtless true, as David Daiches says, that "the credit balance of the New Criticism remains immensely impressive."[131] But when R. W. B. Lewis adds, "The service it has rendered the world of letters in America is incalculable. . . . Its influence, happily, is still strong and salutary,"[132] he is in sharp disagreement with a number of other writers.

. . . most critics . . . are snobs and will only preach to the converted.[133]

Since the wave of reaction which has broken over the world, American poetry has fallen into the hands of a coalition of pedagogues in night caps (whose origin must be sought afar at Vanderbilt), and old, paranoid stalinists. . . .[134]

Poets as well as readers were heard to mutter . . . that poetry was being strangled by criticism, or "internalized," made inaccessible, unpalatable, put . . . completely out of touch with the world that is not poetry.[135]

Remarkably, almost all those who object strongly to "modern" poetry with its symbolist heritage, and to New Criticism with its obsession for analysis, express a powerful yearning for a different kind of poetry—a poetry very like the kind Prévert writes.

. . . there might one day appear a writer to supply the in-touch-with-living authenticity which current American poetry so badly needs, grown as it has genteel and almost suffocatingly proper.[136]

But what I would like to see in new English poetry is a deeper spontaneity, a more trustful and less constricting attitude towards the feelings.[137]

The next few years may well see an important new expansion of poetry, clear and direct in form, unafraid of imagery, losing nothing in personal integrity but linked with the wider issues, the whole-hearted engagements, that can fertilize, deepen and extend the poet's world.[138]

Sometimes, in fact, American poets admit that the stimulus for this new kind of verse may very well come from literature in another language.

Well, I think that for about 20 or 25 years, American poetry has been out of touch with the current poetry being done in Europe. A certain kind of poetry has grown up there which is able to handle the experiences of modern life, including war and advertising and so on, better than any American poets have been able to do.[139]

. . . we must look to writing in other languages than English for the creative joie de vivre that poetry must above all embody: to the poems of a thousand young Frenchmen full of sentimentalities at which Brooks and Warren might laugh, but which come out of an unselfconsciousness that enables these writers to use their imagination at full stretch, resulting in poems that are as far as anything could possibly be from the constipated verses we are accustomed to reading, with their carefully market-tested and approved kind of significance.[140]

Poetry like Prévert's, these comments suggest, may be one of the remedies necessary to cure the self-imposed sterility of modern poetry. If so, the remedy will be administered by prescriptive critics like Shapiro, Jeffers, Hough, and Dickey—critics who believe the great poet of the future will "break sharply from the directions that are fashionable in contemporary poetic literature" and will write a poetry that is "natural and direct."[141]

Prévert has his faults, but they are not as notable as his success, and they in no way mitigate the implicit challenge of his poetry to American criticism. For this Frenchman, with his poetry from the back streets of Paris, poses, against the old dogmas of obscurity, emotion purged by irony, and detachment, a new set of virtues: simplicity, humor for its own sake, unadulterated ire and affection. In Prévert's work, poetry becomes something it has not been in America for some time. It becomes a voice, a shout in fact, of protest against injustice. It becomes the sincere, straightforward expression of passion. It becomes the chronicle of contemporary life at its humblest. With Prévert, in short, poetry becomes human.

Appendix

Appendix

Ceux qui pieusement . . .
Ceux qui copieusement . . .
Ceux qui tricolorent
Ceux qui inaugurent
Ceux qui croient
Ceux qui croient croire
Ceux qui croa-croa
Ceux qui ont des plumes
Ceux qui grignotent
Ceux qui andromaquent
Ceux qui dreadnoughtent
Ceux qui majusculent
Ceux qui chantent en mesure
Ceux qui brossent à reluire
Ceux qui ont du ventre
Ceux qui baissent les yeux
Ceux qui savent découper le poulet
Ceux qui sont chauves à l'intérieur de la tête
Ceux qui bénissent les meutes
Ceux qui font les honneurs du pied
Ceux qui debout les morts
Ceux qui baïonnette . . . on
Ceux qui donnent des canons aux enfants
Ceux qui donnent des enfants aux canons
Ceux qui flottent et ne sombrent pas
Ceux qui ne prennent pas Le Pirée pour un homme
Ceux que leurs ailes de géants empêchent de voler
Ceux qui plantent en rêve des tessons de bouteille sur la grande
    muraille de Chine
Ceux qui mettent un loup sur leur visage quand ils mangent du
    mouton
Ceux qui volent des oeufs et qui n'osent pas les faire cuire

Ceux qui ont quatre mille huit cent dix mètres de Mont Blanc, trois cents de Tour Eiffel, vingt-cinq centimètres de tour de poitrine et qui en sont fiers

Ceux qui mamellent de la France

Ceux qui courent, volent et nous vengent, tous ceux-là, et beaucoup d'autres, entraient fièrement à l'Élysée en faisant craquer les graviers, tous ceux-là se bousculaient, se dépêchaient, car il y avait un grand dîner de têtes et chacun s'était fait celle qu'il voulait.

L'un une tête de pipe en terre, l'autre une tête d'amiral anglais; il y en avait avec des têtes de boule puante, des têtes de Galliffet, des têtes d'animaux malades de la tête, des têtes d'Auguste Comte, des têtes de Rouget de Lisle, des têtes de Sainte Thérèse, des têtes de fromage de tête, des têtes de pied, des têtes de monseigneur et des têtes de crémier.

Quelques-uns, pour faire rire le monde, portaient sur leurs épaules de charmants visages de veaux, et ces visages étaient si beaux et si tristes, avec les petites herbes vertes dans le creux des oreilles comme le goémon dans le creux des rochers, que personne ne les remarquait.

Une mère à tête de morte montrait en riant sa fille à tête d'orpheline au vieux diplomate ami de la famille qui s'était fait la tête de Soleilland.

C'était véritablement délicieusement charmant et d'un goût si sûr que lorsque arriva le Président avec une somptueuse tête d'oeuf de Colomb ce fut du délire.

"C'était simple, mais il fallait y penser", dit le Président en dépliant sa serviette et devant tant de malice et de simplicité les invités ne peuvent maîtriser leur émotion; à travers des yeux cartonnés de crocodile un gros industriel verse de véritables larmes de joie, un plus petit mordille la table, de jolies femmes se frottent les seins très doucement et l'amiral, emporté par son enthousiasme, boit sa flûte de champagne par le mauvais côté, croque le pied de la flûte et l'intestin perforé, meurt debout, cramponné au bastingage de sa chaise en criant: "Les enfants d'abord!"

Étrange hasard, la femme du naufragé, sur les conseils de sa bonne, s'était, le matin même, confectionné une étonnante tête de veuve de guerre, avec les deux grands plis d'amertume de chaque côté de la bouche, et les deux petites poches de la douleur, grises sous les yeux bleus.

Dressée sur sa chaise, elle interpelle le Président et réclame à grands cris l'allocation militaire et le droit de porter sur sa robe du soir le sextant du défunt en sautoir.

Un peu calmée elle laisse ensuite son regard de femme seule errer sur la table et, voyant parmi les hors-d'oeuvre des filets de harengs, elle en prend machinalement en sanglotant, puis en reprend, pensant à l'amiral qui n'en mangeait pas si souvent de son vivant et qui pourtant les aimait tant. Stop. C'est le chef du protocole qui dit qu'il faut s'arrêter de manger, car le Président va parler.

Le Président s'est levé, il a brisé le sommet de sa coquille avec son couteau pour avoir moins chaud, un tout petit peu moins chaud.

Il parle et le silence est tel qu'on entend les mouches voler et qu'on les entend si distinctement voler qu'on n'entend plus du tout le Président parler, et c'est bien regrettable parce qu'il parle des mouches, précisément, et de leur incontestable utilité dans tous les domaines et dans le domaine colonial en particulier.

". . . Car sans les mouches, pas de chasse-mouches, sans chasse-mouches pas de dey d'Alger, pas de consul . . . pas d'affront à venger, pas d'oliviers, pas d'Algérie, pas de grandes chaleurs, messieurs, et les grandes chaleurs, c'est la santé des voyageurs, d'ailleurs . . ."

Mais quand les mouches s'ennuient elles meurent, et toutes ces histoires d'autrefois, toutes ces statistiques les emplissant d'une profonde tristesse, elles commencent par lâcher une patte du plafond, puis l'autre, et tombent comme des mouches, dans les assiettes . . . sur les plastrons, mortes comme le dit la chanson.

"La plus noble conquête de l'homme, c'est le cheval, dit le Président . . . et s'il n'en reste qu'un, je serai celui-là."

C'est la fin du discours; comme une orange abîmée lancée très fort contre un mur par un gamin mal élevé, la MARSEILLAISE éclate et tous les spectateurs éclaboussés par le vert-de-gris et les cuivres, se dressent congestionnés, ivres d'Histoire de France et de Pontet-Canet.

Tous sont debout, sauf l'homme à tête de Rouget de Lisle qui croit que c'est arrivé et qui trouve qu'après tout ce n'est pas si mal exécuté et puis, peu à peu, la musique s'est calmée et la mère à tête de morte en a profité pour pousser sa petite fille à tête d'orpheline du côté du Président.

Les fleurs à la main, l'enfant commence son compliment: "Monsieur le Président . . ." Mais l'émotion, la chaleur, les mouches, voilà qu'elle chancelle et qu'elle tombe le visage dans les fleurs, les dents serrées comme un sécateur.

L'homme à tête de bandage herniaire et l'homme à tête de phlegmon se précipitent, et la petite est enlevée, autopsiée et reniée par sa mère, qui, trouvant sur le carnet de bal de l'enfant des dessins obscènes comme on n'en voit pas souvent, n'ose penser que c'est le diplomate ami de la famille et dont dépend la situation du père qui s'est amusé si légèrement.

Cachant le carnet dans sa robe, elle se pique le sein avec le petit crayon blanc et pousse un long hurlement, et sa douleur fait peine à voir à ceux qui pensent qu'assurément voilà bien là la douleur d'une mère qui vient de perdre son enfant.

Fière d'être regardée, elle se laisse aller, elle se laisse écouter, elle gémit, elle chante:

"Où donc est-elle ma petite fille chérie, où donc est-elle ma petite Barbara qui donnait de l'herbe aux lapins et des lapins aux cobras?"

Mais le Président, qui sans doute n'en est pas à son premier enfant perdu, fait un signe de la main et la fête continue.

Et ceux qui étaient venus pour vendre du charbon et du blé vendent du charbon et du blé et de grandes îles entourées d'eau de tous côtés, de grandes îles avec des arbres à pneus et des pianos métalliques bien stylés pour qu'on n'entende pas trop les cris des indigènes autour des plantations quand les colons facétieux essaient après dîner leur carabine à répétition.

Un oiseau sur l'épaule, un autre au fond du pantalon pour le faire rôtir, l'oiseau, un peu plus tard à la maison, les poètes vont et viennent dans tous les salons.

"C'est, dit l'un d'eux, réellement très réussi." Mais dans un nuage de magnésium le chef du protocole est pris en flagrant délit, remuant une tasse de chocolat glacé avec une cuiller à café.

"Il n'y a pas de cuiller spéciale pour le chocolat glacé, c'est insensé, dit le préfet, on aurait dû y penser, le dentiste a bien son davier, le papier son coupe-papier et les radis roses leurs raviers."

Mais soudain tous de trembler car un homme avec une tête d'homme est entré, un homme que personne n'avait invité et qui pose doucement sur la table la tête de Louis XVI dans un panier.

C'est vraiment la grande horreur, les dents, les vieillards et les portes claquent de peur.

"Nous sommes perdus, nous avons décapité un serrurier," hurlent en glissant sur la rampe d'escalier les bourgeois de Calais dans leur chemise grise comme le cap Gris-Nez.

La grande horreur, le tumulte, le malaise, la fin des haricots, l'état de siège et dehors en grande tenue les mains noires sous les gants blancs, le factionnaire qui voit dans les ruisseaux du sang et sur sa tunique une punaise pense que ça va mal et qu'il faut s'en aller s'il en est encore temps.

"J'aurais voulu, dit l'homme en souriant, vous apporter aussi les restes de la famille impériale qui repose, parait-il, au caveau Caucasien, rue Pigalle, mais les Cosaques qui pleurent, dansent et vendent à boire veillent jalousement leurs morts.

Appendix

"On ne peut pas tout avoir, je ne suis pas Ruy Blas, je ne suis pas Cagliostro, je n'ai pas la boule de verre, je n'ai pas le marc de café. Je n'ai pas la barbe en ouate de ceux qui prophétisent. J'aime beaucoup rire en société, je parle ici pour les grabataires, je monologue pour les débardeurs, je phonographe pour les splendides idiots des boulevards extérieurs et c'est tout à fait par hasard si je vous rends visite dans votre petit intérieur.

"Premier qui dit: et ta soeur, est un homme mort. Personne ne le dit, il a tort, c'était pour rire.

"Il faut bien rire un peu et si vous vouliez, je vous emmènerais visiter la ville mais vous avez peur des voyages, vous savez ce que vous savez et que la Tour de Pise est penchée et que le vertige vous prend quand vous vous penchez vous aussi à la terrasse des cafés.

"Et pourtant vous vous seriez bien amusés, comme le Président quand il descend dans la mine, comme Rodolphe au tapis franc quand il va voir le chourineur, comme lorsque vous étiez enfant et qu'on vous emmenait au Jardin des Plantes voir le grand tamanoir.

"Vous auriez pu voir les truands sans cour des miracles, les lépreux sans cliquette et les hommes sans chemise couchés sur les bancs, couchés pour un instant, car c'est défendu de rester là un peu longtemps.

"Vous auriez vu les hommes dans les asiles de nuit faire le signe de la croix pour avoir un lit, et les familles de huit enfants 'qui crèchent à huit dans une chambre' et, si vous aviez été sages, vous auriez eu la chance et le plaisir de voir le père qui se lève parce qu'il a sa crise, la mère qui meurt doucement sur son dernier enfant, le reste de la famille qui s'enfuit en courant et qui pour échapper à sa misère, tente de se frayer un chemin dans le sang.

"Il faut voir, vous dis-je, c'est passionnant, il faut voir à l'heure où le bon Pasteur conduit ses brebis à la Villette, à l'heure où le fils de famille jette avec un bruit mou sa gourme sur le trottoir, à l'heure où les enfants qui s'ennuient changent de lit dans leur dortoir, il faut voir l'homme couché dans son lit-cage à l'heure où son réveil va sonner.

"Regardez-le, écoutez-le ronfler, il rêve, il rêve qu'il part en voyage, rêve que tout va bien, rêve qu'il a un coin, mais l'aiguille du réveil rencontre celle du train et l'homme levé plonge la tête dans la cuvette d'eau glacée si c'est l'hiver, fétide si c'est l'été.

"Regardez-le se dépêcher, boire son café-crème, entrer à l'usine, travailler, mais il n'est pas encore réveillé, le réveil n'a pas sonné assez fort, le café n'était pas assez fort, il rêve encore, rêve qu'il est en voyage, rêve qu'il a un coin, se penche par la portière et tombe dans

[137]

un jardin, tombe dans un cimetière, se réveille et crie comme une bête, deux doigts lui manquent, la machine l'a mordu, il n'était pas là pour rêver et comme vous pensez ça devait arriver.

"Vous pensez même que ça n'arrive pas souvent et qu'une hirondelle ne fait pas le printemps, vous pensez qu'un tremblement de terre en Nouvelle-Guinée n'empêche pas la vigne de pousser en France, les fromages de se faire et la terre de tourner.

"Mais je ne vous ai pas demandé de penser; je vous ai dit de regarder, d'écouter, pour vous habituer, pour n'être pas surpris d'entendre craquer vos billards le jour où les vrais éléphants viendront reprendre leur ivoire.

"Car cette tête si peu vivante que vous remuez sous le carton mort, cette tête blême sous le carton drôle, cette tête avec toutes ses rides, toutes ses grimaces instruites, un jour vous la hocherez avec un air détaché du tronc et, quand elle tombera dans la sciure, vous ne direz ni oui ni non.

"Et si ce n'est pas vous, ce sera quelques-uns des vôtres, car vous connaissez les fables avec vos bergers et vos chiens, et, ce n'est pas la vaisselle cérébrale qui vous manque.

"Je plaisante, mais vous savez, comme dit l'autre, un rien suffit à changer le cours des choses. Un peu de fulmicoton dans l'oreille d'un monarque malade et le monarque explose. La reine accourt à son chevet. Il n'y a pas de chevet. Il n'y a plus de palais. Tout est plutôt ruine et deuil. La reine sent sa raison sombrer. Pour la réconforter, un inconnu, avec un bon sourire, lui donne le mauvais café. La reine en prend, la reine en meurt et les valets collent des étiquettes sur les bagages des enfants. L'homme au bon sourire revient, ouvre la plus grande malle, pousse les petits princes dedans, met le cadenas à la malle, la malle à la consigne et se retire en se frottant les mains.

"Et quand je dis, Monsieur le Président, Mesdames, Messieurs: le Roi, la Reine, les petits princes, c'est pour envelopper les choses, car on ne peut pas raisonnablement blâmer les régicides qui n'ont pas de roi sous la main, s'ils exercent parfois leurs dons dans leur entourage immédiat.

"Particulièrement parmi ceux qui pensent qu'une poignée de riz suffit à nourrir toute une famille de Chinois pendant de longues années.

"Parmi celles qui ricanent dans les expositions parce qu'une femme noire porte dans son dos un enfant noir et qui portent depuis six ou sept mois dans leur ventre blanc un enfant blanc et mort.

"Parmi les trente mille personnes raisonnables composées d'une âme et d'un corps, qui défilèrent le Six Mars à Bruxelles, musique militaire en tête, devant le monument élevé au Pigeon-Soldat et parmi celles qui défileront demain à Brive-la-Gaillarde, à Rosa-la-Rose ou à Carpa-la-Juive, devant le monument du Jeune et veau marin qui périt à la guerre comme tout un chacun . . ."

Mais une carafe lancée de loin par un colombophile indigné touche en plein front l'homme qui racontait comment il aimait rire. Il tombe. Le Pigeon-Soldat est vengé. Les cartonnés officiels écrasent la tête de l'homme à coups de pied et la jeune fille, qui trempe en souvenir le bout de son ombrelle dans le sang, éclate d'un petit rire charmant. Le musique reprend.

La tête de l'homme est rouge comme une tomate trop rouge, au bout d'un nerf un oeil pend, mais sur le visage démoli, l'oeil vivant, le gauche, brille comme une lanterne sur des ruines.

"Emportez-le," dit le Président, et l'homme couché sur une civière et le visage caché par une pèlerine d'agent sort de l'Élysée horizontalement, un homme derrière lui, un autre devant.

"Il faut bien rire un peu," dit-il au factionnaire et le factionnaire le regarde passer avec ce regard figé qu'ont parfois les bons vivants devant les mauvais.

Découpée dans le rideau de fer de la pharmacie une étoile de lumière brille et, comme des rois mages en mal d'enfant Jésus, les garçons bouchers, les marchands d'édredons et tous les hommes de coeur contemplent l'étoile qui leur dit que l'homme est à l'intérieur, qu'il n'est pas tout à fait mort, qu'on est en train peut-être de le soigner et tous attendent qu'il sorte avec l'espoir de l'achever.

Ils attendent, et bientôt, à quatre pattes à cause de la trop petite ouverture du rideau de fer, le juge d'instruction pénètre dans la boutique, le pharmacien l'aide à se relever et lui montre l'homme mort, la tête appuyée sur le pèse-bébé.

Et le juge se demande, et le pharmacien regarde le juge se demander si ce n'est pas le même homme qui jeta des confetti sur le corbillard du maréchal et qui, jadis, plaça la machine infernale sur le chemin du petit caporal.

Et puis ils parlent de leurs petites affaires, de leurs enfants, de leurs bronches; le jour se lève, on tire les rideaux chez le Président.

Dehors, c'est le printemps, les animaux, les fleurs, dans les bois de Clamart on entend les clameurs des enfants qui se marrent, c'est le printemps, l'aiguille s'affole dans sa boussole, le binocard entre au bocard et la grande dolichocéphale sur son sofa s'affale et fait la folle.

Il fait chaud. Amoureuses, les allumettes-tisons se vautrent sur leur frottoir, c'est le printemps, l'acné des collégiens et voilà la fille du

sultan et le dompteur de mandragores, voilà les pélicans, les fleurs
sur les balcons, voilà les arrosoirs, c'est la belle saison.

Le soleil brille pour tout le monde, il ne brille pas dans les prisons,
il ne brille pas pour ceux qui travaillent dans la mine,
ceux qui écaillent le poisson
ceux qui mangent la mauvaise viande
ceux qui fabriquent les épingles à cheveux
ceux qui soufflent vides les bouteilles que d'autres boiront pleines
ceux qui coupent le pain avec leur couteau
ceux qui passent leurs vacances dans les usines
ceux qui ne savent pas ce qu'il faut dire
ceux qui traient les vaches et ne boivent pas le lait
ceux qu'on n'endort pas chez le dentiste
ceux qui crachent leurs poumons dans le métro
ceux qui fabriquent dans les caves les stylos avec lesquels d'autres
    écriront en plein air que tout va pour le mieux
ceux qui en ont trop à dire pour pouvoir le dire
ceux qui ont du travail
ceux qui n'en ont pas
ceux qui en cherchent
ceux qui n'en cherchent pas
ceux qui donnent à boire aux chevaux
ceux qui regardent leur chien mourir
ceux qui ont le pain quotidien relativement hebdomadaire
ceux qui l'hiver se chauffent dans les églises
ceux que le suisse envoie se chauffer dehors
ceux qui croupissent
ceux qui voudraient manger pour vivre
ceux qui voyagent sous les roues
ceux qui regardent la Seine couler
ceux qu'on engage, qu'on remercie, qu'on augmente, qu'on diminue,
    qu'on manipule, qu'on fouille, qu'on assomme
ceux dont on prend les empreintes
ceux qu'on fait sortir des rangs au hasard et qu'on fusille
ceux qu'on fait défiler devant l'Ark
ceux qui ne savent pas se tenir dans le monde entier
ceux qui n'ont jamais vu la mer
ceux qui sentent le lin parce qu'ils travaillent le lin
ceux qui n'ont pas l'eau courante
ceux qui sont voués au bleu horizon
ceux qui jettent le sel sur la neige moyennant un salaire absolument
    dérisoire

ceux qui vieillissent plus vite que les autres
ceux qui ne se sont pas baissés pour ramasser l'epingle
ceux qui crèvent d'ennui le dimanche après-midi
    parce qu'ils voient venir le lundi
    et le mardi, et le mercredi, et le jeudi, et le vendredi,
    et le samedi
    et le dimanche après-midi.

LA GRASSE MATINÉE

Il est terrible
le petit bruit de l'oeuf dur cassé sur un comptoir d'étain
il est terrible ce bruit
quand il remue dans la mémoire de l'homme qui a faim
elle est terrible aussi la tête de l'homme
la tête de l'homme qui a faim
quand il se regarde à six heures du matin
dans la glace du grand magasin
une tête couleur de poussière
ce n'est pas sa tête pourtant qu'il regarde
dans la vitrine de chez Potin
il s'en fout de sa tête l'homme
il n'y pense pas
il songe
il imagine une autre tête
une tête de veau par exemple
avec une sauce de vinaigre
ou une tête de n'importe quoi qui se mange
et il remue doucement la mâchoire
doucement
et il grince des dents doucement
car le monde se paye sa tête
et il ne peut rien contre ce monde
et il compte sur ses doigts un deux trois
un deux trois
cela fait trois jours qu'il n'a pas mangé
et il a beau se répéter depuis trois jours
Ça ne peut pas durer

ça dure
trois jours
trois nuits
sans manger
et derrière ces vitres
ces pâtés ces bouteilles ces conserves
poissons morts protégés par les boîtes
boîtes protégées par les vitres
vitres protégées par les flics
flics protégés par la crainte
que de barricades pour six malheureuses sardines ...
Un peu plus loin le bistro
café-crème et croissants chauds
l'homme titube
et dans l'intérieur de sa tête
un brouillard de mots
un brouillard de mots
sardines à manger
oeuf dur café-crème
café arrosé rhum
café-crème
café-crème
café-crime arrosé sang! ...
Un homme très estimé dans son quartier
a été égorgé en plein jour
l'assassin le vagabond lui a volé
deux francs
soit un café arrosé
zéro franc soixante-dix
deux tartines beurrées
et vingt-cinq centimes pour le pourboire du garçon.

Il est terrible
le petit bruit de l'oeuf dur cassé sur un comptoir d'étain
il est terrible ce bruit
quand il remue dans la mémoire de l'homme qui a faim.

RIVIERA

Assise sur une chaise longue
une dame à la langue fanée
une dame longue
plus longue que sa chaise longue
et très âgée
prend ses aises
on lui a dit sans doute que la mer était là
alors elle la regarde
mais elle ne la voit pas
et les présidents passent et la saluent très bas
c'est la baronne Crin
la reine de la carie dentaire
son mari c'est le baron Crin
le roi du fumier de lapin
et tous à ses grands pieds sont dans leurs petits souliers
et ils passent devant elle et la saluent très bas
de temps en temps
elle leur jette un vieux cure-dents
ils le sucent avec ravissement
en continuant leur promenade
leurs souliers neufs craquent et leurs vieux os aussi
et des villas arrive une musique blême
une musique aigre
et sure
comme les cris d'un nouveau-né trop longtemps négligé
c'est nos fils
c'est nos fils disent les présidents
et ils hochent la tête doucement et fièrement
et leurs petits prodiges
désespérément
se jettent à la figure leurs morceaux de piano
la baronne prête l'oreille
cette musique lui plaît
mais son oreille tombe
comme une vieille tuile d'un toit
elle regarde par terre
et elle ne la voit pas
mais l'aperçoit seulement
et la prend

tout bonnement
pour une feuille morte apportée par le vent
c'est alors que s'arrête
la triste clameur des enfants
que la baronne n'entendait plus d'ailleurs
que d'une oreille distraite
et dépareillée
et que surgissent brusquement
gambadent dans sa pauvre tête
en toute liberté
les vieux refrains puérils méchants et périmés
de sa mémoire inquiète usée et déplumée
et comme elle cherche vainement
pour passer le temps
qui la menace et qui la guette
un bon regret bien triste et bien attendrissant
qui puisse la faire rire aux larmes
ou même pleurer tout simplement
elle ne trouve qu'un souvenir incongru inconvenant
l'image d'une vielle dame assise toute nue
sur la bosse d'un chameau
et qui tricote méchamment une omelette au guano.

LE RETOUR AU PAYS

C'est un Breton qui revient au pays natal
Après avoir fait plusieurs mauvais coups
Il ne reconnaît personne
Personne ne le reconnaît
Il est très triste.
Il entre dans une crêperie pour manger des crêpes
Mais il ne peut pas en manger
Il a quelque chose qui les empêche de passer
Il paye
Il sort
Il allume une cigarette
Mais il ne peut pas la fumer.
Il y a quelque chose
Quelque chose dans sa tête
Quelque chose de mauvais

Il est de plus en plus triste
Et soudain il se met à se souvenir:
Quelqu'un lui a dit quand il était petit
"Tu finiras sur l'échafaud"
Et pendant des années
Il n'a jamais osé rien faire
Pas même traverser la rue
Pas même partir sur la mer
Rien absolument rien.
Il se souvient.
Celui qui avait tout prédit c'est l'oncle Grésillard
L'oncle Grésillard qui portait malheur à tout le monde
La vache!
Et le Breton pense à sa soeur
Qui travaille à Vaugirard
A son frère mort à la guerre
Pense à toutes les choses qu'il a vues
Toutes les choses qu'il a faites.
La tristesse se serre contre lui
Il essaie une nouvelle fois
D'allumer une cigarette
Mais il n'a pas envie de fumer
Alors il décide d'aller voir l'oncle Grésillard.
Il y va
Il ouvre la porte
L'oncle ne le reconnaît pas
Mais lui le reconnaît
Et il lui dit:
"Bonjour oncle Grésillard"
Et puis il lui tord le cou.
Et il finit sur l'échafaud à Quimper
Après avoir mangé deux douzaines de crêpes
Et fumé une cigarette.

FAMILIALE

La mère fait du tricot
Le fils fait la guerre
Elle trouve ça tout naturel la mère
Et le père qu'est-ce qu'il fait le père?
Il fait des affaires
Sa femme fait du tricot
Son fils la guerre
Lui des affaires
Il trouve ça tout naturel le père
Et le fils et le fils
Qu'est-ce qu'il trouve le fils?
Il ne trouve rien absolument rien le fils
Le fils sa mère fait du tricot son père des affaires lui la guerre
Quand il aura fini la guerre
Il fera des affaires avec son père
La guerre continue la mère continue elle tricote
Le père continue il fait des affaires
Le fils est tué il ne continue plus
Le père et la mère vont au cimetière
Ils trouvent ça tout naturel le père et la mère
La vie continue la vie avec le tricot la guerre les affaires
Les affaires la guerre le tricot la guerre
Les affaires les affaires et les affaires
La vie avec le cimetière.

BARBARA

Rappelle-toi Barbara
Il pleuvait sans cesse sur Brest ce jour-là
Et tu marchais souriante
Épanouie ravie ruisselante
Sous la pluie
Rappelle-toi Barbara
Il pleuvait sans cesse sur Brest
Et je t'ai croisée rue de Siam
Tu souriais
Et moi je souriais de même

Rappelle-toi Barbara
Toi que je ne connaissais pas
Toi qui ne me connaissais pas
Rappelle-toi
Rappelle-toi quand même ce jour-là
N'oublie pas
Un homme sous un porche s'abritait
Et il a crié ton nom
Barbara
Et tu as couru vers lui sous la pluie
Ruisselante ravie épanouie
Et tu t'es jetée dans ses bras
Rappelle-toi cela Barbara
Et ne m'en veux pas si je te tutoie
Je dis tu à tous ceux que j'aime
Même si je ne les ai vus qu'une seule fois
Je dis tu à tous ceux qui s'aiment
Même si je ne les connais pas
Rappelle-toi Barbara
N'oublie pas
Cette pluie sage et heureuse
Sur ton visage heureux
Sur cette ville heureuse
Cette pluie sur la mer
Sur l'arsenal
Sur le bateau d'Ouessant
Oh Barbara
Quelle connerie la guerre
Qu'es-tu devenue maintenant
Sous cette pluie de fer
De feu d'acier de sang
Et celui qui te serrait dans ses bras
Amoureusement
Est-il mort disparu ou bien encore vivant
Oh Barbara
Il pleut sans cesse sur Brest
Comme il pleuvait avant
Mais ce n'est plus pareil et tout est abîmé
C'est une pluie de deuil terrible et désolée
Ce n'est même plus l'orage
De fer d'acier de sang
Tout simplement des nuages

Qui crèvent comme des chiens
Des chiens qui disparaissent
Au fil de l'eau sur Brest
Et vont pourrir au loin
Au loin très loin de Brest
Dont il ne reste rien.

POUR TOI MON AMOUR

Je suis allé au marché aux oiseaux
Et j'ai acheté des oiseaux
Pour toi
mon amour
Je suis allé au marché aux fleurs
Et j'ai acheté des fleurs
Pour toi
mon amour
Je suis allé au marché à la ferraille
Et j'ai acheté des chaînes
De lourdes chaînes
Pour toi
mon amour
Et puis je suis allé au marché aux esclaves
Et je t'ai cherchée
Mais je ne t'ai pas trouvée
mon amour.

ALICANTE

Une orange sur la table
Ta robe sur le tapis
Et toi dans mon lit
Doux présent du présent
Fraîcheur de la nuit
Et j'ai acheté des chaînes
Chaleur de ma vie.

Quartier Libre

J'ai mis mon képi dans la cage
et je suis sorti avec l'oiseau sur la tête
Alors
on ne salue plus
a demandé le commandant
Non
on ne salue plus
a répondu l'oiseau
Ah bon
excusez-moi je croyais qu'on saluait
a dit le commandant
Vous êtes tout excusé tout le monde peut se tromper
a dit l'oiseau.

Il ne Faut Pas . . .

Il ne faut pas laisser les intellectuels jouer avec les
allumettes
Parce que Messieurs quand on le laisse seul
Le monde mental Messssieurs
N'est pas du tout brillant
Et sitôt qu'il est seul
Travaille arbitrairement
S'érigeant pour soi-même
Et soi-disant généreusement en l'honneur des travailleurs
du bâtiment
Un auto-monument
Répétons-le Messssssieurs
Quand on le laisse seul
Le monde mental
Ment
Monumentalement.

PAGE D'ÉCRITURE

Deux et deux quatre
quatre et quatre huit
huit et huit font seize . . .
Répétez! dit le maître
Deux et deux quatre
quatre et quatre huit
huit et huit font seize.
Mais voilà l'oiseau-lyre
qui passe dans le ciel
l'enfant le voit
l'enfant l'entend
l'enfant l'appelle:
Sauve-moi
joue avec moi
oiseau!
Alors l'oiseau descend
et joue avec l'enfant
Deux et deux quatre . . .
Répétez! dit le maître
et l'enfant joue
l'oiseau joue avec lui . . .
Quatre et quatre huit
huit et huit font seize
et seize et seize qu'est-ce qu'ils font?
Ils ne font rien seize et seize
et surtout pas trente-deux
de toute façon
et ils s'en vont.
Et l'enfant a caché l'oiseau
dans son pupitre
et tous les enfants
entendent sa chanson
et tous les enfants
entendent la musique
et huit et huit à leur tour s'en vont
et quatre et quatre et deux et deux
à leur tour fichent le camp
et un et un ne font ni une ni deux
un à un s'en vont également.

Et l'oiseau-lyre joue
et l'enfant chante
et le professeur crie:
Quand vous aurez fini de faire le pitre!
Mais tous les autres enfants
écoutent la musique
et les murs de la classe
s'écroulent tranquillement.
Et les vitres redeviennent sable
l'encre redevient eau
les pupitres redeviennent arbres
la craie redevient falaise
le porte-plume redevient oiseau.

DANS MA MAISON

Dans ma maison vous viendrez
D'ailleurs ce n'est pas ma maison
Je ne sais pas à qui elle est
Je suis entré comme ça un jour
Il n'y avait personne
Seulement des piments rouges accrochés au mur blanc
Je suis resté longtemps dans cette maison
Personne n'est venu
Mais tous les jours et tous les jours
Je vous ai attendue

Je ne faisais rien
C'est-à-dire rien de sérieux
Quelquefois le matin
Je poussais des cris d'animaux
Je gueulais comme un âne
De toutes mes forces
Et cela me faisait plaisir
Et puis je jouais avec mes pieds
C'est très intelligent les pieds
Ils vous emmènent très loin
Quand vous voulez allez très loin
Et puis quand vous ne voulez pas sortir
Ils restent là ils vous tiennent compagnie

Et quand il y a de la musique ils dansent
On ne peut pas danser sans eux
Faut être bête comme l'homme l'est si souvent
Pour dire des choses aussi bêtes
Que bête comme ses pieds gai comme un pinson
Le pinson n'est pas gai
Il est seulement gai quand il est gai
Et triste quand il est triste ou ni gai ni triste
Est-ce qu'on sait ce que c'est un pinson
D'ailleurs il ne s'appelle pas réellement comme ça
C'est l'homme qui a appelé cet oiseau comme ça
Pinson pinson pinson pinson

Comme c'est curieux les noms
Martin Hugo Victor de son prénom
Bonaparte Napoléon de son prénom
Pourquoi comme ça et pas comme ça
Un troupeau de bonapartes passe dans le désert
L'empereur s'appelle Dromadaire
Il a un cheval caisse et des tiroirs de course
Au loin galope un homme qui n'a que trois prénoms
Il s'appelle Tim-Tam-Tom et n'a pas de grand nom
Un peu plus loin encore il y a n'importe qui
Beaucoup plus loin encore il y a n'importe quoi
Et puis qu'est-ce que ça peut faire tout ça

Dans ma maison tu viendras
Je pense à autre chose mais je ne pense qu'à ça
Et quand tu seras entrée dans ma maison
Tu enlèveras tous tes vêtements
Et tu resteras immobile nue debout avec ta bouche rouge
Comme les piments rouges pendus sur le mur blanc
Et puis tu te coucheras et je me coucherai près de toi
Voilà
Dans ma maison qui n'est pas ma maison tu viendras.

Appendix

POUR FAIRE LE PORTRAIT D'UN OISEAU

Peindre d'abord une cage
avec une porte ouverte
peindre ensuite
quelque chose de joli
quelque chose de simple
quelque chose de beau
quelque chose d'utile
pour l'oiseau
placer ensuite la toile contre un arbre
dans un jardin
dans un bois
ou dans une forêt
se cacher derrière l'arbre
sans rien dire
sans bouger . . .
Parfois l'oiseau arrive vite
mais il peut aussi bien mettre de longues années
avant de se décider
Ne pas se décourager
attendre
attendre s'il le faut pendant des années
la vitesse ou la lenteur de l'arrivée de l'oiseau
n'ayant aucun rapport
avec la réussite du tableau
Quand l'oiseau arrive
s'il arrive
observer le plus profond silence
attendre que l'oiseau entre dans la cage
et quand il est entré
fermer doucement la porte avec le pinceau
puis
effacer un à un tous les barreaux
en ayant soin de ne toucher aucune des plumes de
    l'oiseau
Faire ensuite le portrait de l'arbre
en choisissant la plus belle de ses branches
pour l'oiseau
peindre aussi le vert feuillage et la fraîcheur du vent
la poussière du soleil

et le bruit des bêtes de l'herbe dans la chaleur de l'été
et puis attendre que l'oiseau se décide à chanter
Si l'oiseau ne chante pas
c'est mauvais signe
signe que le tableau est mauvais
mais s'il chante c'est bon signe
signe que vous pouvez signer
Alors vous arrachez tout doucement
une des plumes de l'oiseau
et vous écrivez votre nom dans un coin du tableau.

LANTERNE MAGIQUE DE PICASSO

Tous les yeux d'une femme joués sur le même tableau
Les traits de l'être aimé traqué par le destin sous la fleur immobile
    d'un sordide papier peint
L'herbe blanche du meurtre dans une forêt de chaises
Un mendiant de carton éventré sur une table de marbre
Les cendres d'un cigare sur le quai d'une gare
Le portrait d'un portrait
Le mystère d'un enfant
La splendeur indéniable d'un buffet de cuisine
La beauté immédiate d'un chiffon dans le vent
La folle terreur du piège dans un regard d'oiseau
L'absurde hennissement d'un cheval décousu
La musique impossible des mules à grelots
Le taureau mis à mort couronné de chapeaux
La jambe jamais pareille d'une rousse endormie et la très grande
    oreille de ses moindres soucis
Le mouvement perpétuel attrapé à la main
L'immense statue de pierre d'un grain de sel marin
La joie de chaque jour et l'incertitude de mourir et le fer de l'amour
    dans la plaie d'un sourire
La plus lointaine étoile du plus humble des chiens
Et salé sur une vitre le tendre goût du pain
La ligne de chance perdue et retrouvée brisée et redressée parée des
    haillons bleus de la nécessité
L'étourdissante apparition d'un raisin de Malaga sur un gâteau de riz
Un homme dans un bouge assommant à coups de rouge le mal du
    pays

Et la lueur aveuglante d'un paquet de bougies
Une fenêtre sur la mer ouverte comme une huître
Le sabot d'un cheval le pied nu d'une ombrelle
La grâce incomparable d'une tourterelle toute seule dans une maison
très froide
Le poids mort d'une pendule et ses moments perdus
Le soleil somnambule qui réveille en sursaut au milieu de la nuit la
Beauté somnolente et soudain éblouie qui jette sur ses épaules le
manteau de la cheminée et l'entraîne avec lui dans le noir de
fumée masquée de blanc d'Espagne et vêtue de papiers collés
Et tant de choses encore
Une guitare de bois vert berçant l'enfance de l'art
Un ticket de chemin de fer avec tous ses bagages
La main qui dépayse un visage qui dévisage un paysage
L'écureuil caressant d'une fille neuve et nue
Splendide souriante heureuse et impudique
Surgissant à l'improviste d'un casier à bouteilles ou d'un casier à
musique comme une panoplie de plantes vertes vivaces et
phalliques
Surgissant elle aussi à l'improviste du tronc pourrissant
D'un palmier académique nostalgique et désespérément vieux beau
comme l'antique
Et les cloches à melon du matin brisées par le cri d'un journal du soir
Les terrifiantes pinces d'un crabe émergeant des dessous d'un panier
La dernière fleur d'un arbre avec les deux gouttes d'eau du condamné
Et la mariée trop belle seule et abandonnée sur le divan cramoisi de
la jalousie par la blême frayeur de ses premiers maris
Et puis dans un jardin d'hiver sur le dossier d'un trône une chatte en
émoi et la moustache de sa queue sous les narines d'un roi
La chaux vive d'un regard dans le visage de pierre d'une vieille
femme assise près d'un panier d'osier
Et crispées sur le minium tout frais du garde-fou d'un phare tout blanc
les deux mains bleues de froid d'un Arlequin errant qui regarde la
mer et ses grands chevaux dormant dans le soleil couchant et puis
qui se réveillent les naseaux écumants les yeux phosphorescents
affolés par la lueur du phare et ses épouvantables feux tournants
Et l'alouette toute rôtie dans la bouche d'un mendiant
Une jeune infirme folle dans un jardin public qui souriant d'un sourire
déchiré mécanique en berçant dans ses bras un enfant léthargique
trace dans la poussière de son pied sale et nu la silhouette du père
et ses profils perdus et présente aux passants son nouveau-né en
loques Regardez donc mon beau regardez donc ma belle ma

merveille des merveilles mon enfant naturel d'un côté c'est un
garçon et de l'autre c'est une fille tous les matins il pleure mais
tous les soirs je la console et je les remonte comme une pendule
Et aussi le gardien du square fasciné par le crépuscule
La vie d'une araignée suspendue à un fil
L'insomnie d'une poupée au balancier cassé et ses grands yeux de
verre ouverts à tout jamais
La mort d'un cheval blanc la jeunesse d'un moineau
La porte d'une école rue du Pont-de-Lodi
Et les Grands Augustins empalés sur la grille d'une maison dans une
petite rue dont ils portent le nom
Tous les pêcheurs d'Antibes autour d'un seul poisson
La violence d'un oeuf la détresse d'un soldat
La présence obsédante d'une clef cachée sous un paillasson
Et la ligne de mire et la ligne de mort dans la main autoritaire et
potelée d'un simulacre d'homme obèse et délirant camouflant
soigneusement derrière les bannières exemplaires et les crucifix
gammés drapés et dressés spectaculairement sur le grand balcon
mortuaire du musée des horreurs et des honneurs de la guerre la
ridicule statue vivante des ses petites jambes courtes et de son
buste long mais ne parvenant pas malgré son bon sourire de
Caudillo grandiose et magnanime à cacher les irrémédiables et
pitoyables signes de la peur de l'ennui de la haine et de la connerie
gravés sur son masque de viande fauve et blême comme les graffiti
obscènes de la mégalomanie gravés par les lamentables tortionnaires
de l'ordre nouveau dans les urinoirs de la nuit
Et derrière lui dans le charnier d'une valise diplomatique entr'ouverte
le cadavre tout simple d'un paysan pauvre assailli dans son champ
à coups de lingots d'or par d'impeccables hommes d'argent
Et tout à côté sur une table une grenade ouverte avec toute une ville
dedans
Et toute la douleur de cette ville rasée et saignée à blanc
Et toute la garde civile caracolant tout autour d'une civière
Où rêve encore un gitan mort
Et toute la colère d'un peuple amoureux travailleur insouciant et
charmant qui soudain éclate brusquement comme le cri rouge d'un
coq égorgé publiquement
Et le spectre solaire des hommes aux bas salaires qui surgit tout
sanglant des sanglantes entrailles d'une maison ouvrière tenant à
bout de bras la pauvre lueur de la misère la lampe sanglante de
Guernica et découvre au grand jour de sa lumière crue et vraie les
épouvantables fausses teintes d'un monde décoloré usé jusqu'à la

corde vidé jusqu'à la moelle
D'un monde mort sur pied
D'un monde condamné
Et déjà oublié
Noyé carbonisé aux mille feux de l'eau courante du ruisseau populaire
Ou le sang populaire court inlassablement
Intarissablement
Dans les artères et dans les veines de la terre et dans les artères et
    dans les veines de ses véritables enfants
Et le visage de n'importe lequel de ses enfants dessiné simplement
    sur une feuille de papier blanc
Le visage d'André Breton le visage de Paul Éluard
Le visage d'un charretier aperçu dans la rue
La lueur du clin d'oeil d'un marchand de mouron
Le sourire épanoui d'un sculpteur de marrons
Et sculpté dans le plâtre un mouton de plâtre frisé bêlant de vérité
    dans la main d'un berger de plâtre debout près d'un fer à repasser
A côté d'une boîte à cigares vide
A côté d'un crayon oublié
A côté des Métamorphoses d'Ovide
A côté d'un lacet de soulier
A côté d'un fauteuil aux jambes coupées par la fatigue des années
A côté d'un bouton de porte
A côté d'une nature morte où les rêves enfantins d'une femme de
    ménage agonisent sur la pierre froide d'un évier comme des pois-
    sons suffoquant et crevant sur des galets brûlants
Et la maison remuée de fond en comble par les pauvres cris de pois-
    son mort de la femme de ménage désespérée tout à coup qui fait
    naufrage soulevée par les lames de fond du parquet et va s'échouer
    lamentablement sur les bords de la Seine dans les jardins du Vert-
    Galant
Et là désemparée elle s'assoit sur un banc
Et elle fait ses comptes
Et elle ne se voit pas blanche pourrie par les souvenirs et fauchée
    comme les blés
Une seule pièce lui reste une chambre à coucher
Et comme elle va la jouer à pile ou face avec le vain espoir de gagner
    un peu de temps
Un grand orage éclate dans la glace à trois faces
Avec toutes les flammes de la joie de vivre
Tous les éclairs de la chaleur animale
Toutes les lueurs de la bonne humeur

Et donnant le coup de grâce à la maison désorientée
Incendie les rideaux de la chambre à coucher
Et roulant en boule de feu les draps au pied du lit
Découvre en souriant devant le monde entier
Le puzzle de l'amour avec tous ses morceaux
Tous ses morceaux choisis par Picasso
Un amant sa maîtresse et ses jambes à son cou
Et les yeux sur les fesses les mains un peu partout
Les pieds levés au ciel et les seins sens dessus dessous
Les deux corps enlacés échangés caressés
L'amour décapité délivré et ravi
La tête abandonnée roulant sur le tapis
Les idées délaissées oubliées égarées
Mises hors d'état de nuire par la joie et le plaisir
Les idées en colère bafouées par l'amour en couleur
Les idées terrées et atterrées comme les pauvres rats de la mort
    sentant venir le bouleversant naufrage de l'Amour
Les idées remises à leur place à la porte de la chambre à côté du pain
    à côté des souliers
Les idées calcinées escamotées volatilisées désidéalisées
Les idées pétrifiées devant la merveilleuse indifférence d'un monde
    passionné
D'un monde retrouvé
D'un monde indiscutable et inexpliqué
D'un monde sans savoir-vivre mais plein de joie de vivre
D'un monde sobre et ivre
D'un monde triste et gai
Tendre et cruel
Réel et surréel
Terrifiant et marrant
Nocturne et diurne
Solite et insolite
Beau comme tout.

INVENTAIRE

Une pierre
deux maisons
trois ruines
quatre fossoyeurs
un jardin
des fleurs

un raton laveur

une douzaine d'huîtres un citron un pain
un rayon de soleil
une lame de fond
six musiciens
une porte avec son paillasson
un monsieur décoré de la légion d'honneur

un autre raton laveur

un sculpteur qui sculpte des Napoléon
la fleur qu'on appelle souci
deux amoureux sur un grand lit
un receveur des contributions une chaise trois dindons
un ecclésiastique un furoncle
une guêpe
un rein flottant
une écurie de courses
un fils indigne deux frères dominicains trois sauterelles un strapontin
deux filles de joie un oncle Cyprien
une Mater dolorosa trois papas gâteau deux chèvres de Monsieur
    Seguin
un talon Louis XV
un fauteuil Louis XVI
un buffet Henri II deux buffets Henri III trois buffets Henri IV
un tiroir dépareillé
une pelote de ficelle deux épingles de sûreté un monsieur âgé
une Victoire de Samothrace un comptable deux aides-comptables un
    homme du monde deux chirurgiens trois végétariens
un cannibale
une expédition coloniale un cheval entier une demi-pinte de bon sang
    une mouche tsé-tsé
un homard à l'américaine un jardin à la française

deux pommes à l'anglaise
un face-à-main un valet de pied un orphelin un poumon d'acier
un jour de gloire
une semaine de bonté
un mois de Marie
une année terrible
une minute de silence
une seconde d'inattention
et . . .

cinq ou six ratons laveurs

un petit garçon qui entre à l'école en pleurant
un petit garçon qui sort de l'école en riant
une fourmi
deux pierres à briquet
dix-sept éléphants un juge d'instruction en vacances assis sur un pliant
un paysage avec beaucoup d'herbe verte dedans
une vache
un taureau
deux belles amours trois grandes orgues un veau marengo
un soleil d'Austerlitz
un siphon d'eau de Seltz
un vin blanc citron
un Petit Poucet un grand pardon un calvaire de pierre une échelle de
    corde
deux sœurs latines trois dimensions douze apôtres mille et une nuits
    trente-deux positions six parties du monde cinq points cardinaux
    dix ans de bons et loyaux services sept péchés capitaux deux doigts
    de la main dix gouttes avant chaque repas trente jours de prison
    dont quinze de cellule cinq minutes d'entr'acte

et . . .

plusieurs ratons laveurs.

TOURNESOL

Tous les jours de la semaine
En hiver en automne
Dans le ciel de Paris
Les cheminées d'usine ne fument que du gris

Mais le printemps s'amène une fleur sur l'oreille
Au bras une jolie fille
Tournesol Tournesol
C'est le nom de la fleur
Le surnom de la fille
Elle n'a pas de grand nom pas de nom de famille
Et danse au coin des rues
A Belleville à Séville

Tournesol Tournesol Tournesol
Valse des coins de rues
Et les beaux jours sont venus
La belle vie avec eux
Le génie de la Bastille fume une gitane bleue
Dans le ciel amoureux
Dans le ciel de Séville dans le ciel de Belleville
Et même de n'importe où

Tournesol Tournesol
C'est le nom de la fleur
Le surnom de la fille.

Déjeuner du Matin

Il a mis le café
Dans la tasse
Il a mis le lait
Dans la tasse de café
Il a mis le sucre
Dans le café au lait
Avec la petite cuiller
Il a tourné
Il a bu le café au lait
Et il a reposé la tasse
Sans me parler
Il a allumé
Une cigarette
Il a fait des ronds
Avec la fumée
Il a mis les cendres
Dans le cendrier
Sans me parler
Sans me regarder
Il s'est levé
Il a mis
Son chapeau sur sa tête
Il a mis
Son manteau de pluie
Parce qu'il pleuvait
Et il est parti
Sous la pluie
Sans une parole
Sans me regarder
Et moi j'ai pris
Ma tête dans ma main
Et j'ai pleuré.

Notes and References

Notes and References

Preface

1. Letter from the Librairie Gallimard, December 10, 1964.
2. Jean Queval, *Jacques Prévert*, Mercure de France (Paris, 1955), 9.
3. Edmond Humeau, "Jacques Prévert parmi nous," *Sortilèges 3 et 4*, Nouvelle Thouars (Paris, 1952), 54.
4. Bernard Fay, *Panorama de la littérature contemporaine*, Editions KRA (Paris, 1952), 216.
5. Thierry Maulnier (pseud. for Jacques Talagrand), *Introduction à la poésie française*, Gallimard (Paris, 1939), 39.
6. Maulnier, 40.
7. Gaetan Picon, *Panorama de la nouvelle littérature française*, Gallimard (Paris, 1949), 178–79.
8. Raymond Queneau, "Jacques Prévert," *Revue de Paris* (juin, 1951), 41.
9. Pierre Brodin, *Présences contemporaines*, Debresse (Paris, 1954), 25.
10. Kenneth Cornell, "French Literature since World War II: Criticism and Research," *Symposium*, XI, no. 1 (Spring, 1957), passim.
This paper, presented in December, 1956, purportedly—and probably does—review French and American criticism of French poetry after 1945. It makes no mention of Prévert. Similarly, Wallace Fowlie's *Mid-Century French Poets* (1955) ignores Prévert. Such an omission would be unthinkable in France.
11. Queval, 13.

Chapters 1–3

1. Eliot G. Fay, "The Poetry of Jacques Prévert," *The Emory University Quarterly*, II, no. 4 (Dec., 1947), 232.
2. Raymond Queneau, "Jacques Prévert," *Revue de Paris* (juin, 1951), 45.
3. See "Gens de Viet Nam . . . ," *La pluie et le beau temps*.

4. Jean Queval, *Jacques Prévert*, Mercure de France (Paris, 1955).

5. Queval, 109.

6. Gaetan Picon, *Panorama de la nouvelle littérature française*, Librairie Gallimard (Paris, 1949), 191.

7. Queval, 13.

Dinner of Heads

A. An allusion to Victor Hugo's well-known poem *Hymne*, which begins "Ceux qui pieusement sont morts pour la patrie. . . ."

B. Priests are sometimes called "corbeaux" (crows) in France.

C. The motto of Paris is *Fluctuat nec mergitur*; I substituted an allusion, roughly comparable in emotional value, to American history.

D. Probably an echo from Baudelaire's poem *L'Albatros*, 1. 16.

E. Sully, minister under Henry IV, said "Labourage et pâturage sont les deux mamelles de la France." The slogan has always been popular among conservative, landed aristocrats.

F. A line from Corneille's *Le Cid*, I, vi, 290. Don Diègue is urging his son Don Rodrigue to avenge an affront to the father's honor.

G. Gallifet (Gaston Alexandre Auguste) was a French general and, eventually, minister of war, notorious for his harsh suppression of the Paris Commune in 1871.

H. A pun on the title of one of La Fontaine's fables, *Les Animaux malades de la peste*.

I. Soleilland comitted a famous, horrible crime; he murdered and dismembered a little girl.

J. A reference to the famous incident of the slap with a fly swatter, given by the Dey, Hussein, to the French Consul Deval on April 30, 1827. This insult precipitated a blockade of Algiers, which in turn led eventually to the French invasion and conquest of North Africa.

K. Composer of the "Marseillaise" (1792).

L. "Le mauvais café" means in current slang "a dose of poison."

M. A small city in south-central France; symbol of provincialism much as Boise, Idaho, might be in the United States.

N. A pun on Carpe à la Juive, a dish of carp in cold jelly, composed of latin *carpa* (sic), meaning "seize" and la Juive (the Jewess).

8. *Paroles*, 16.

9. *Paroles*, 17.

10. *Paroles*, 189.

Notes and References

11. *Paroles*, 85.
12. Queval, 200.
13. Queval, 215.
14. See Gaston Bouthol, "J. P. et un siècle de poésie martiale," *Lettres Nouvelles*, no. 56 (1958), 96.

In an otherwise adequate account of Prévert's treatment of war, this writer also refuses to credit the poet with any "enthousiasme combattant."

15. *Paroles*, 15.
16. *Paroles*, 136.
17. *Paroles*, 135.
18. *Paroles*, 36.
19. Queval, 191.
20. Queval, 186.
21. Queval, 193.
22. Queval, 193.
23. *Paroles*, 142.
24. Queval, 187–88.
25. Queval, 144.
26. Queval, 151. See also Fay, 450.
27. *Paroles*, 158.
28. *Paroles*, 76.
29. *Paroles*, 76.
30. *Spectacle*, 61.
31. Serge Brindeau, in "Jacques Prévert parmi nous," *Sortilèges*, *3 et 4*, Nouvelle Thoars (Paris, 1952), 51.
32. William Wordsworth, *Poetical Works*, ed. Ernest de Selincourt, vol. 4, Clarendon Press (Oxford, 1947), 57.
33. Noel Arnaud, *Sortilèges*, 49.
34. Alfred H. Barr, ed. *Picasso: Forty Years of His Art*, Museum of Modern Art (New York, 1939), 18.
35. Barr, 18.
36. Barr, 10.

Chapters 4–7

1. Charles Edward Gauss, *The Aesthetic Theories of French Artists*, Johns Hopkins Press (Baltimore, 1949), 81.
2. Gauss, 83.
3. Jean-Louis Bédouin, *André Breton*, Série: "Poètes d'Aujourd'hui," Éditions Pierre Seghers (Paris, 1955), 114.

4. C[ecil] M[aurice] Bowra, *The Heritage of Symbolism,* Macmillan & Co. (London, 1943). See also Arthur Symons, *The Symbolist Movement in Literature,* Rev. and enl. ed., E. P. Dutton and Co. (New York, 1919). The attitude is by no means moribund in French letters: cf. Robert Kanters, "Vous ne comprenez plus nos poètes," *Le Figaro Littéraire* (avril 23, 1960), 1, 5.

5. Wallace Fowlie, *Age of Surrealism,* Swallow Press (New York, 1950), 15.

6. André Billy, *Max Jacob,* Série: "Poètes d'Aujourd'hui," Éditions Pierre Seghers (Paris, 1956), 42.

7. Marcel Raymond, *From Baudelaire to Surrealism,* trans. G. M., Wittenborn, Schultz, Inc. (New York, 1949), 67.

8. Picon, 131.

9. Picon, 131.

10. Queval, 228.

11. Bédouin, 23. See also Christiane Burucoa, *Sortilèges,* 8.

12. Bédouin, 25.

13. Fowlie, 43.

14. Fowlie, 22.

15. Fowlie, 88, and Billy, 40.

16. Billy, 94.

17. Billy, 89.

18. *Paroles,* 268.

19. Billy, 30.

20. Léon-Gabriel Gros, "Poètes Contemporains" *Cahiers du Sud* (1951), 200.

21. Bataille, 205.

22. Bataille, 206.

23. Queval, 39.

24. Maurice Nadeau, *Littérature présente,* Éditions Corea (Paris, 1952), 321.

25. Raymond, 279.

26. Raymond, 286.

27. Queval, 48.

28. Gros, 201.

29. Gros, 201.

30. Queval, 50.

31. Fay, 236.

32. *Paroles,* 133.

33. Albert Gaudin, "La Poésie de Jacques Prévert," *French Review,* XX (May, 1947), 431.

34. Claude Roy, quoted in Queval, 33.

35. Gaudin, 435.

36. Criticus (pseud. for Marcel Berger), *Le style au Microscope,* Calmann-Levy (Paris, 1951), 175 ff.

37. Eugenio de Andrade, *Sortilèges,* 21.

38. Gaudin, 436.

39. Bataille, 196. For a more thorough discussion of Prévert as a song writer, see Georges Mounin, "Poésie et chanson populaire," *Les Temps Modernes,* no. 122 (fevr., 1956), 1329.

40. Queval, 42–43. The point is amplified in Caradec, "Les Livres pour enfants de Jacques Prévert," *Lettres Nouvelles,* no. 1 (mars, 1953), 109.

41. Maurice Rat, "J. P.," *l'Éducation Nationale,* no. 25 (Oct. 6, 1955), 10–11.

42. Quoted in Queval, 53.

43. Queval, 53 ff.

44. Gaudin, 432.

45. Gaudin, 433–34.

46. Gaudin, 434.

47. Nadeau, 326. cf. J. Thomas, "Grammaire et poésie: Le Message de Jacques Prévert," *Le Français Moderne,* XXVI, 126.

48. Picon, 193.

49. Nadeau, 322.

50. Queval, 38.

51. Queval, 56.

52. Gros, 126.

53. Gaudin, 429.

Chapter 8

1. Robert Bly, "On English and American Poetry," *The Fifties,* II, no. 2 (1959), 47.

2. Ferlinghetti published *Selections from Paroles* as number 9 in his "Pocket Poets Series" (1958), but he was reading Prévert poems in various San Francisco night clubs as early as 1955. (Letter from Frank Jones, Comparative Literature Department, University of Washington.) A glance at Ferlinghetti's own work, *Pictures of the Gone World* (1955) and *A Coney Island of the Mind* (1957), reveals a number of parallels between his style and Prévert's. The San Francisco poet's "Tentative Description of a Dinner to Promote the Impeachment of President Eisenhower" must certainly derive from Prévert's "Tentative de description d'un dîner de têtes. . . ."

3. René Taupin, *l'Influence du symbolisme français sur la poésie américaine*, Librairie Ancienne Honoré Champion (Paris, 1929), 288.

4. For J. Isaacs, in *The Background of English Poetry*, E. P. Dutton and Co. (New York, 1952), "modern poetry" and "laforgian poetry" are almost interchangeable.

5. René Huyghe, "Delacroix and Baudelaire," *Arts Yearbook*, Doubleday & Co. (New York, 1958), 35.

6. George E[douard] Lemaître, *From Cubism to Surrealism in French Literature*, Harvard University Press (Cambridge, 1941), 16.

7. Lemaître, 214.

8. Franz Alexander, "The Psychoanalyst Looks at Contemporary Art," *Art and Psychoanalysis*, Criterion Books (New York, 1957), 360.

9. Frank Kermode, *Romantic Image*, Routledge and Kegan Paul (London, 1957), 153.

10. Huyghe, 41.

11. Claude Vigée, "Metamorphoses of Modern Poetry," *Comparative Literature*, VII, no. 2 (Spring, 1955), 192.

12. Kermode, 108.

13. Arthur Symons, *The Symbolist Movement in Literature*, Rev. and enl. ed., E. P. Dutton and Co. (New York, 1919), 182.

14. Symons, 203.

15. Marcel Raymond, *From Baudelaire to Surrealism*, trans. G. M., Wittenborn, Schultz, Inc. (New York, 1949), 23.

16. Raymond, 23.

17. Raymond, 23.

18. R. P. Blackmur, "The American Literary Expatriate," in *Foreign Influences in American Life*, Princeton University Press (Princeton, 1944), 126–45.

18a. Randall Jarrell, "The Obscurity of the Poet," *Partisan Review*, XVIII (1951), 68–81.

18b. Archibald MacLeish, "The Isolation of the American Artist," *Atlantic*, CCI (January, 1958), 55–59.

18c. Delmore Schwartz, "The Isolation of Modern Poetry," *Kenyon Review*, III (Summer, 1945), 209–220.

18d. Stephen Spender, "Are Poets out of Touch with Life?" *The Listener*, LXVIII (Sept. 20, 1962), 439.

19. Kimon Friar and John Malcolm Brinnin, eds., *Modern Poetry: American and British*, Appleton-Century-Crofts, Inc. (New York, 1951), 421.

20. Cleanth Brooks, *Modern Poetry and the Tradition*, University of North Carolina Press (Chapel Hill, 1939), 60.

21. Symons, 210.

22. Elizabeth Drew, *Directions in Modern Poetry*, W. W. Norton & Co. (New York, 1940), 28.

23. MacLeish, 59 (See 18b).

24. Robert E. Spiller, "Literature and the Critics," *American Perspectives: The National Self-Image in the Twentieth Century.* ed. Robert E. Spiller and Eric Larrabee, Harvard University Press (Cambridge, 1961), 50–51.

25. Henry Popkin, "The Larger Audience," *A Time of Harvest: American Literature 1910–1960.*, ed. Robert E. Spiller (New York, 1962), 122.

26. William Van O'Connor, *Sense and Sensibility in Modern Poetry*, University of Chicago Press (Chicago, 1948), 251.

27. Wallace Fowlie, *Mid-Century French Poets*, Grove Press (New York, 1955), 11.

28. Guy Michaud, *Message poétique du Symbolisme*, 4 vols., Librairie Nizet (Paris, 1947), 337–38.

29. Raymond, 123.

30. Raymond, 27.

31. Babette Deutsch, *Poetry in Our Time*, Henry Holt & Co. (New York, 1952), 180–81.

32. Bly, 46. cf. M. L. Rosenthal, *The Modern Poets: A Critical Introduction*, Oxford University Press (New York, 1960), 5.

33. Deutsch, 167.

34. Deutsch, 154.

35. Deutsch, 154.

36. T[homas] S[tearns] Eliot, *Selected Essays*, Harcourt, Brace and Company (New York, 1932), 6–7.

37. Eliot, 10.

38. Louise Bogan, *Achievement in American Poetry*, Gateway Editions, Inc. (New York, 1951), 6.

39. Eliot, 248.

40. Drew, 204.

41. Isaacs, 20.

42. Bogan, 65.

43. Brooks, 60.

44. John Press, *The Chequer'd Shade: Reflections on Obscurity in Poetry*, Oxford University Press (London, 1958), 204.

45. Jarrell, 66 (See 18a).

46. O'Connor, 227.

47. Herbert Read, *The Nature of Literature*, Grove Press, Inc. (New York, ?), 99.

48. Press, 214.

49. Robert Conquest, "Mistah Eliot—He Dead?" *Audit*, I, no. ii (March 28, 1960), 13.

50. Read, *Nature*, 100.

51. John Crowe Ransom, *The New Criticism*, New Directions (Connecticut, 1941), 3.

52. Stanley Edgar Hyman, *The Armed Vision*, Alfred A. Knopf, Inc. (New York, 1948), 10–11.

53. Walter Sutton, *Modern American Criticism*, Prentice-Hall (New Jersey, 1963), 3–4.

54. Raymond, 350–51.

55. Raymond, 349.

56. Hyman, 63.

57. Eliot, 249.

58. C. M. Bowra, *The Creative Experiment*, Macmillan & Co. (London, 1949), 27.

59. Hyman, 72.

60. Shelton J. Lachman, *The Foundations of Science*, The Hamilton Press (Detroit, 1956), 36.

61. I[vor] A[rmstrong] Richards, *Principles of Literary Criticism*, Harcourt, Brace and Co. (New York, 1924), 61.

62. Spender, *Listener*, 439.

63. Richards, 61.

64. William J. Handy, "Science, Literature, and Modern Criticism," *Texas Quarterly*, I, no. 2 (Spring, 1958), 149.

65. O'Connor, 156.

66. John Crowe Ransom, "Criticism as Pure Speculation," *Literary Opinion in America*, ed. M. D. Zabel, Harper (New York, 1951), 648.

67. Spiller, 57.

68. Murray Krieger, *The New Apologists for Poetry*, Indiana University Press (Bloomington, 1963), 200.

69. Irving Howe, "Modern Criticism in America," *Nation*, vol. CLXXXVII (1958), 390.

70. Isaacs, 18.

71. Raymond, 35.

72. Richards, 25.

73. Richards, 25.

74. Ray B[enedict] West, ed., *Modern Literary Criticism*, Rinehart & Company, Inc. (New York, 1952), 325.

75. David Daiches, *Poetry and the Modern World*, University of Chicago Press (Chicago, 1940), 112.

76. Drew, 80–81.

77. Bogan, 72.

78. Bogan, 85.
79. Ransom, 16.
80. Kermode, 116.
81. Bogan, 69.
82. Hyman, 11.
83. Hyman, 7.
84. Bogan, 100.
85. Malcolm Cowley, "The Religion of Art: The Death of a Religion," *The New Republic* (New York, January 17, 1934), 272.
86. Raymond, 252.
87. Anna E[lizabeth] Balakian, *Literary Origins of Surrealism,* King's Crown Press (New York, 1947), 73.
88. Lemaître, 180.
89. Albert Thibaudet, *Histoire de la littérature française,* Librairie Stock (Paris, 1936), 486.
90. Bowra, *Heritage,* 29.
91. Henri Clouard, *Histoire de la littérature française,* Albin Michel (Paris, 1949), 25.
92. Souday, Paul, *Paul Valéry,* "Les Documentaires," Simon Kra (Paris, 1927), 19.
93. Read, *Nature,* 97.
94. Raymond, 154.
95. Cowley, 273.
96. Maulnier, 50.
97. Thibaudet, 487.
98. Lemaître, 21.
99. Lemaître, 21.
100. Raymond, 31.
101. Clouard, 147; cf. Pierre Brodin, *Présences contemporaines* (Paris, 1954), 16.
102. Clouard, 147.
103. Vigée, 112; cf. Jean Rousselot, *Panorama critique des nouveaux poètes français,* Pierre Seghers (Paris, 1952), 68.
104. Lemaître, 198.
105. Brodin, 16.
106. Picon, 28.
107. Picon, 28.
108. Bataille, 196.
109. Picon, 22–23.
110. Brodin, 25.
111. Paul Saintaux, *Sortilèges,* 27.
112. Richards, 36.

113. Brooks, 2–3.

114. Fowlie, *Mid-Century*, 19.

115. Wallace Fowlie, "French Poetry Today," *Poetry*, CIV, no. 5 (August, 1964), 322.

116. *Ibid.*, 323.

117. *Ibid.*, 323.

118. *Ibid.*, 323.

119. Deutsch, 53–54.

120. Daiches, 240–41.

121. H. R. Hays, "Surrealist Influence in Contemporary English and American Poetry," *Poetry*, LIV, no. 4 (July, 1939), 204.

122. F. O. Matthiessen, "The Responsibilities of the Critic," *Visions and Revisions in Modern Literary Criticism*, ed. Bernard S. Oldsey and Arthur O. Lewis, Jr. E. P. Dutton & Co., Inc. (New York, 1962), 167. Says Matthiessen, "In too many recent articles literature seems to be regarded as a puzzle to be solved."

123. Kermode, 164.

124. Vigée, 103.

125. Hyman, 57.

126. Drew, 198–99. This radical statement of the position appears in Richard K. Barksdale, "Trends in Contemporary Poetry," *Phylon*, XIX (Winter, 1958), 415: "Finally, contemporary poetry is filled with extreme emotional reticence. All laughter and tears are carefully cloaked in cryptic parentheses; and even sex, the dominant twentieth-century emotion, is described with clinical brevity. None of the modern poets luxuriate in their emotions."

127. Paul Goodman, "Advance-Guard Writing, 1900–1950," *Kenyon Review*, XIII, no. 3 (Summer, 1951), 371.

128. James Dickey, *The Suspect in Poetry*, The Sixties Press (Madison, 1964), 10.

129. Karl Shapiro, "T. S. Eliot: The Death of Literary Judgment," *Saturday Review* (February 27, 1960), 15.

130. Graham Hough, *Reflections on a Literary Revolution*, Catholic University Press (Washington, D.C., 1960), 65.

131. David Daiches, "The New Criticism," *A Time of Harvest: American Literature 1910–1960*, ed. Robert Spiller (New York, 1962), 109–10.

132. R. W. B. Lewis, "American Letters: A Projection," *Yale Review*, LI (1961), 215.

133. Louis MacNeice, "Poetry, the Public, and the Critic," *The New Statesman and Nation*, vol. 38 (Oct. 8, 1949), 381.

134. Kenneth Rexroth, "l'Influence de la poésie française sur la poésie américaine," *Europe* (fevrier–mars, 1959), 65.

135. Francis Golffing and Barbara Gibs, "The Public Voice: Remarks on Poetry Today—The Reality of Verse," *Commentary*, XXVIII (1959), 64.

136. Dickey, 17.

137. G. S. Fraser, "English Poetry Since 1945," *London Magazine*, VI, no. 2 (November, 1959), 14.

138. Jack Lindsay, "The Position of English Poets," *Meanjin*, XVII, no. 3 (Spring, 1958), 329. See also Peter Viereck, "The Education of a Poet," *Atlantic*, CLXXXVII (1951), 76.

139. Robert Bly, quoted in *The Sullen Art: Interviews with Modern American Poets*, ed. David Ossman. Corinth Books (New York, 1963), 39.

140. Dickey, 23.

141. Robinson Jeffers, "Poetry and Survival," *Perspectives, U.S.A.*, Intercultural Publications, Inc. (New York, 1953), 103.

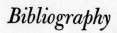

Bibliography

Bibliography

I WORKS BY PRÉVERT (IN CHRONOLOGICAL ORDER)

Paroles, Ed. du Point du Jour, Coll. "Le Calligraphe." Paris, 1946. The first important collection of the poet's work, containing such famous poems as *Dîner de têtes*, *La Crosse en l'air*. It was an immediate success, provoked much critical controversy.

Histoires, in coll. with André Verdet, illustrated by Mayo. Le Pré aux Clercs. Paris, 1946. This small volume contains poems in a somewhat lighter vein than those found in *Paroles*.

Paroles, rev. and enl. ed. Ed. du Point du Jour. Paris, 1947. This is the definitive edition of the book, from which all subsequent printings have been made.

C'est à Saint-Paul-De-Vence . . . , La Nouvelle Edition. Paris, 1949. This long poem is a colorful account of a local festival, expressed as an offhand eulogy to his companion at the celebration, André Verdet.

Spectacle, Le Point du Jour-N.R.F. Paris, 1951. Like *Paroles*, this volume collects work done over previous years. It contains principally dramatic sketches, some performable, others not. One of Prévert's best-known works, *La Bataille de Fontenoy*, is available in this edition.

Vignette pour les vignerons, with sketches by Françoise Gilot and with photographs by Marianne. Ed. Falaize. 1951. A commemorative poem—boldly pagan—for the wine-growers' festival at Saint-Jeannet.

Le Grand Bal du printemps, with photographs by Izis. La Guilde du Livre. Lausanne, 1951. A sustained rhapsody, on Paris and Parisians, rather remarkable in Prévert's work, where satire usually counterbalances joy.

Charmes de Londres, with photographs by Izis. La Guilde du Livre. Lausanne, 1952. Native Londoners might be dumbfounded, and perhaps amused, that a Frenchman could find so much magic in the back streets of their city, but mere visitors will appreciate the poet's unerring eye for the exciting and significant details of a scene new to him.

La Pluie et le beau temps, Le Point du Jour-N.R.F. Paris, 1955. Prévert's third major collection of verse, this volume also contains both recent and older work. It contains a dramatic sketch or two, some songs, and numerous short poems, but nothing of the scope and power of the long poems in *Paroles*.

Miró, in coll. with G. Ribemont-Dessaignes and with reprod. by Miró. Maeght. Paris, 1956. An accolade for one of the poet's favorite painters.

Portraits de Picasso, with photographs by André Villers. Muggiani. Milan, 1959. Another tribute to an old friend, whose work has inspired some of Prévert's own comments on art.

Histoires, et d'autres histoires, new edition. Le Point du Jour-N.R.F. Paris, 1963. An admittedly random assortment of poems, most of them already published in earlier works.

Besides these works, Prévert has written a number of children's books. These are listed below.

Contes pour enfants pas sages, illustrated by Elsa Henriquez. Le Pré aux Clercs. Paris, 1947.

Le Petit Lion, with photographs by Ylla. Arts et Métiers Graphiques. Paris, 1947.

Des bêtes . . . , with photographs by Ylla. Le Point du Jour-N.R.F. Paris, 1950.

Bim, le petit âne, with photographs by Albert Lamorisse. La Guilde du Livre, Lausanne, also Paris, Hachette. 1952.

Lettre des Iles Baladar, with sketches by André François. Le Point du Jour-N.R.F. Paris, 1952.

Guignol, with designs by Elsa Henriquez. La Guilde du Livre. Lausanne, 1952.

Tour de chant, with sketches by Loris and musical score by Christiane Verger. La Guilde du Livre. Lausanne, 1953.

L'Opéra de la lune, with sketches by Jacqueline Duhême and musical score by Christiane Verger. La Guilde du Livre. Lausanne, 1953.

II BOOKS ABOUT PRÉVERT

Jacques Prévert parmi nous. Sortilèges 3 et 4. Paris, 1950. A collection of opinions from other writers, critics and personal friends of the poet. For the most part, these essays are laudatory; but the critics' remarks range from the wildly enthusiastic (Christian Gali, Edmond Humeau) to the equivocal (Paul Chaulot) or even contemptuous (Charles le Quintrec). Some other contributors: Eugenio de Andrade, Noel Arnaud, Jean L'Anselme, Christiane Burucoa, Claudine Chonez, Armand Lanoux, Paul Saintaux, Serge Brindeau.

QUEVAL, JEAN. *Jacques Prévert*. Paris, 1955. The only available full-length study of Prévert's work, this book devotes most attention to his film art. Few poems are discussed in great detail, but there are provocative comments on Prévert's style in general, and one of the few attempts to assess the moral dimensions of his work. One serious shortcoming: The critic fails to appreciate the violence of Prévert's satire.

III   BOOKS CONTAINING REMARKS ON PRÉVERT'S POETRY

BRODIN, PIERRE. *Présences contemporaines*. Paris, 1954. Prévert is discussed here as a leading exponent of the "poetry of revolt." The critic views him, and others like Michaux, Salacrou, Queneau, as an extension of the Dada and Surrealist movements. There is no extensive commentary on specific works.

CRITICUS (pseud. for Marcel Berger). *Le Style au microscope*. Paris, 1951. A more apt title might be "Style through the Wrong End of a Telescope." The section on Prévert contains not close textual analysis, but mere invective. One of the most openly hostile treatments of the poet.

GROS, LÉON-GABRIEL. *Poètes contemporains*. Cahiers du Sud. 1951. Contains an evaluation of the poet's success as a satirist, with special attention to the veiled denunciation of modern life in poems of humorous absurdity (*Inventaire*, *Cortège*).

NADEAU, MAURICE. *Littérature présente*. Paris, 1952. One chapter presents a succinct though not a thorough description of the most salient characteristics of Prévert's style, including some remarks on his "cinematic" quality.

PICON, GAETAN. *Panorama de la nouvelle littérature française*. Paris, 1949. One of the best synoptic accounts of French poetry since 1910. Prévert appears in a chapter entitled "Quatre Poètes Majeurs," where Picon attempts to place him in the context of recent literary history.

ROUSSELOT, JEAN. *Panorama critique des nouveaux poètes français*. Paris, 1952. A cursory three pages on the immediate literary roots of Prévert's work.

ROY, CLAUDE. *Descriptions critiques*. Paris, 1949. Perhaps the shortest and most superficial commentary on the poet, interesting chiefly because Roy has stature as a critic and, even at this early date, recognized *Paroles* as a book of considerable merit.

SAILLET, MAURICE. *Billets doux de Justin Saget*. Paris, 1952. The few remarks directed to Prévert's poetry are friendly applause rather than scholarly criticism.

IV ARTICLES ABOUT PRÉVERT'S POETRY

BATAILLE, GEORGES. "De L'âge de pierre à Jacques Prévert," *Critique*, no. 3–4 (avril–sept., 1946), 195–214. One of the most substantial short pieces on the poet, though often highly speculative. Bataille attempts to trace the special quality of "anti-poetry" to distant origins—the folk ballad, primitive chant, etc. "Poetry turns away from itself at birth." The critic views Prévert as one of those who restores emotional value to language exhausted by an overly rigid literary "tradition."

BOUTHOUL, GASTON. "Jacques Prévert et un siècle de poésie martiale," *Lettres Nouvelles*, no. 56, 91–101. Despite the promising title, this article fails to confront the paradox implicit in Prévert's attitudes toward war and revolution. Overlooking the poet's life-long campaign against the bourgeoisie, the critic says, "Prévert, first of all, provides an example of this new phenomenon: a poet who rejects the zeal of combat."

CARADEC, JEAN, "Les Livres pour enfants de Jacques Prévert," *Lettres Nouvelles*, no. 1 (mars, 1953), 109–111. In the course of his commentary on the children's books, this critic reminds us that Prévert is not a "writer" in the usual sense, but a yarn-spinner, song-writer, and cinema script composer.

CHAVARDES, MAURICE. "Poètes et blasphémateurs," *La Vie Intellectuelle*, no. 10 (oct., 1950), 375–77. A brief discussion of the modern poets' handling of religious matters. Prévert is seen as the dedicated opponent of oppressive religions and the spokesman of a new, tender humanism.

DUMAYET, PIERRE. "Prévert et l'optimism," *Poésie 46*, no. 33 (1946). A brief, appreciatory note from that period when Prévert's first book was one of the few sources of light in a bleak land.

FALIZE, JEAN. "Entrez, entrez Mesdames et Messieurs, voici Jacques Prévert, l'aigre à deux têtes," *Marginales*, no. 18 (jan.–mars, 1950), 266–68. The two heads are poetry and film, and Falize decides that techniques from the two media are inextricably interwoven: Prévert writes cinematic poetry and poetic cinema. The critic objects to what he calls the "esthetic of misery" in some works directed to social problems, but praises Prévert's carefully wrought "artlessness."

FAY, ELIOT. "Bird Poems of Jacques Prévert," *MLJ*, XXXIII, no. 6 (Oct., 1949), 450–57. Fay's articles are notable mostly because they appear to be the first commentary on Prévert to appear in American journals. Despite a lugubrious reading of the light-hearted *Pour faire le portrait d'un oiseau*, this critic rightly looks to the "bird poems" for hints toward an esthetic credo.

————. "The Poetry of Jacques Prévert," *The Emory University Quarterly*, III, no. 4 (Dec., 1947), 231–37. A general, superficial commentary on *Paroles*.

GAUDIN, ALBERT. "La Poésie de Jacques Prévert," *FR*, XX (May, 1947), 423–38. An excellent early survey of the poet's work. Gaudin gives first painstaking attention and then unstinted praise to the variety of stylistic innovations in *Paroles*.

HENRIOT, ÉMILE. "Jacques Prévert et le pouvoir des mots," *Le Monde*, no. 3411 (11 jan., 1956), 7. A member of the Academy, Henriot chastises Prévert severely for his destructive satire and "professional non-conformism," saying "This unserious Prévert comes dangerously near spoiling the other poet in him who knows how to be touching and charming."

MARZARS, PIERRE. "Jacques Prévert serait-il un des créatures de Paris?" *Le Figaro Littéraire* (14 juillet, 1951), 1. A short, qualified, but front-page encomium.

POUJOL, JACQUES. "Jacques Prévert ou le langage en procès," *FR*, XXXI (avril, 1958), 387–95. Comments on Prévert's style, dealing primarily with his inventive uses of "common" speech.

QUENEAU, RAYMOND. "Jacques Prévert," *Revue de Paris* (juin, 1951), 39–46. As usual, this critic's remarks are pungent and provocative. He esteems Prévert and Sartre as the authors who most appeal to the post-war youth of France; both are, he thinks, moralists and stylists of major stature.

RAT, MAURICE. "J. P.," *Éducation Nationale*, no. 25 (6 oct., 1955), 9–12. Brief and obvious. Rat thinks Prévert's poems are more than word games because they possess a "tender anarchism" and an "instinctive rebellion" against a dehumanized society.

THOMAS, J. "Grammaire et poésie: le message de Jacques Prévert," *FM*, XXVI (1958), 124–28. A slightly pedantic note on certain of Prévert's stylistic traits. The author attempts to provide a grammatical model for the camera-like objectivity of some poems.

Index

Index